RAILWAYS OF THE ISLE OF PORTLAND

By
Martin Smith

The principal *raison d'être* for the Portland branch was stone. This is Suckthumb Quarry, about $^3/_4$-mile south-west of Easton between the villages of Weston and Southwell. The workings are advancing from the left of the picture, cutting into the open fields - the field in the upper right part of the picture will soon be excavated, too. What we see behind the 'retaining walls' at the rear of the cranes is largely surface waste - in some parts of Portland, 40ft depth of 'top soil' (forgive the layman's phraseology) had to be removed before the 'proper' stone was reached. This picture was taken in April 1930, at which time the quarry owners, Messrs. F.J. Barnes, had around 100 men working at the site. The quarries were infilled in the late 1980s. (The information about the quarrying aspect in this and other BGS photographs were gleaned from Peter Stanier's excellent book *Quarries of England and Wales*). PHOTOGRAPH: BRITISH GEOLOGICAL SURVEY

Contents

Background iii

1. The 'Merchants Railway' 1
The original 4ft 6in gauge Portland Railway

2. The Weymouth & Portland Railway 5
Early trials and tribulations - and a very unpopular station

3. The Admiralty Line 11
An integral component

4. The Easton & Church Hope Railway 13
Completing the railway map of Portland

5. The Twentieth Century 18
The story from 1900 until 1965

6. The Route 25
Along the line......

7. Locomotives and train services 39
Weymouth to Easton - from 1865 to 1965

Acknowledgements

During the preparation of this modest little book, various railway company documents, Board of Trade files and working timetables were consulted. Secondary sources include *Railways of Dorset* by J.H.Lucking (RCTS 1968), *LSWR Locomotives* by D.L.Bradley, *Track Layout Diagrams of the GWR - Section 17* by R.A.Cooke and G.A.Pryer (privately published), *Quarries of England and Wales* by Peter Stanier (Twelveheads Press 1995), *Railway Bylines* (Vol.2, No.2), and various issues of the *Railway Observer*, the *GWR Magazine*, and the *Railway Magazine*.

    Sincere thanks are due to Messrs. Bryan Wilson, Eric Youldon, Colin Caddy, Richard Casserley, Ray Collins and George Pryer for their invaluable assistance with this project. Thanks also to Dr.Jean Alexander and Tony Morigi of the British Geological Survey for their help and co-operation. The British Geological Survey possesses a large, important UK-wide collection of photographs of rocks, fossils, minerals and geologically related landscape features. Photographic materials date from the early 1900s to the present day. Selected recent materials can be accessed via WorldWideWebb@http://www.nkw.ac.uk/bgs/

First Published in the United Kingdom by
IRWELL PRESS 1997
59A, High Street, Clophill, Bedfordshire MK45 4BE
Printed in Huddersfield by The Amadeus Press

Background

The Isle of Portland, just to the south of Weymouth, has been alternatively described as 'the Gibraltar of Wessex' and 'a scarred, treeless rock'. It could also be accused of having a misleading name, for it is not actually an island. It is linked to the mainland by a narrow causeway of natural origin - the eastern end of the famous Chesil Beach. Furthermore, in 1839 a road bridge - named Ferrybridge - was constructed across the Small Mouth of the East Fleet, thus providing a second permanent link between the 'island' and the mainland.

Portland is roughly 4 miles long and 1³/₄ miles wide. At its northern end it rises abruptly above the community of Fortuneswell to a height of 496ft, but southwards from the summit the plateau slopes gradually down towards Portland Bill, at which point the cliffs are only about 10 feet or so above the sea. The description of Portland as 'scarred and treeless' might seem a little harsh - the village of Easton, with its wide main street and smartly-painted cottages, is, in fact, rather attractive - but everywhere on Portland scenes akin to moonscapes, created by extensive quarrying, are ever present.

Portland has been intermittently quarried for its famous building stone since Roman times. There was a considerable flurry in the fourteenth century, when stone was extracted for such famous buildings as the Tower of London and the Palace of Westminster, but it was in the seventeenth century that the industry really took off. Perhaps the most famous use of Portland stone during this period was in the construction of St. Pauls Cathedral in London, work on which commenced in 1675. Portland stone was a very popular building material in London - liked not only for its smart appearance, but also its resistance to discolouring and weathering. The use of Portland stone in London became so extensive that it has been said - albeit with tongue in cheek - that there is more Portland stone in the capital than there is on Portland itself.

Portland is also well known for its Naval base, which was developed in the 1850s and went on to become an integral part of the community - a role it fulfilled until very recently. Another familiar local establishment is the prison, which was established in the mid-1800s and is still in use today. It has always been considered fairly secure, as escapees have either to traverse the causeway (rather conspicuous) or swim across to Weymouth (very dangerous, due to the treacherous currents). Even when discussing the Naval base and the prison, it is not possible to get away from the subject of quarrying. The breakwaters for Portland Harbour were constructed of Portland stone, and much of the manpower for building the breakwater and extracting the stone came in the form of convict labour, the prison being built specially to house the reluctant workforce. In other words, quarrying has affected everyday life on Portland, directly and indirectly.

None of Portland's quarries was more than a couple of miles or so from a point where the stone could be loaded into sea-going ships, and the advantages of the coastal location were further enhanced in 1826 when a tramway was opened to Castletown Pier, one of the principal points of 'export'. These arrangements sufficed for almost forty years, but were partially superseded in 1865 when Portland became connected to Britain's 'main line' railway network. In 1900 the railway was extended to Easton, a focal point of the local quarrying industry, and this enabled Portland stone to be taken directly from the central quarries and stone workshops to destinations throughout Britain.

The story of Portland's quarrying industry and its railways became so closely intertwined although, somewhat ironically perhaps, the peak period for quarrying on Portland was in the 1890s - rather *before* the arrival of the railway at Easton. The boom of the 1890s was due to the construction of a new breakwater at Portland Harbour - massive quantities of local stone were required, and this provided employment for well over a thousand men. During the early part of the 1900s there were usually around 500-600 men involved in quarrying, but in the early 1930s the number rose again, peaking at about 900.

Portland's railway history is a fascinating subject, not least because of its comparative complexity. Even before the nineteenth century was out, no less than five different railway companies and a Government department had been involved in the development of just nine miles of railway. The intrigue didn't cease with the completion of Portland's railway map in the early 1900s. The two principal local companies - the Weymouth & Portland Railway and the Easton & Church Hope Railway - continued as fully independent concerns until the end of 1947, despite never having owned or operated one locomotive, passenger carriage or goods wagon between them throughout their entire corporate lives.

The Isle of Portland has often been described as having an independent air, borne largely of remoteness and isolation. As we shall see, Portland's railways had a similarly remote and independent air...

Ivatt 2-6-2T No.41305 hauls a fairly substantial Portland branch goods through Melcombe Regis station - disused but still intact - on 16 February 1965. PHOTOGRAPH: COLIN CADDY

Top. Easton Stone Works, April 1930. This building is alongside Park Road at Easton, and still stands today. PHOTOGRAPH: BRITISH GEOLOGI-CAL SURVEY

Below. An O2 0-4-4T pulls out of Easton with a train for Weymouth. The loco appears to be either No.188 or 189 - if it is the latter, the date of the picture can be narrowed down to pre-July 1933, in which month it was withdrawn. Indeed, a date no later than the 1930s would be in order, as the original footbridge is still *in situ*.

Chapter One
The 'Merchants Railway'

In the early nineteenth century there was an increasing demand for Portland stone, and by 1824 around 27,000 tons were being exported by sea from Portland each year. This prompted local quarry owners to propose a public tramway between the quarries and the shipping piers at Portland Castle, and authorisation for the tramway was granted in 1825. To put this event into its proper perspective, this was the same year in which the world-famous Stockton & Darlington Railway was opened to traffic, and over *thirty years* before the town of Weymouth had a railway. Portland's very first railway was an extremely early pioneer in its field, but that status has been widely overlooked. The railway's relative obscurity is undoubtedly due - at least in part - to the fact that it was worked by a combination of horse power and a cable-worked incline. Being devoid of locomotives, the line did not attract the widespread attention it deserved. Such obscurity, on the face of it, is wholly unjust.

Although referred to locally as the 'Merchants Railway' or the 'Freemans Incline', the official title of the enterprise was the Portland Railway. It was promoted by local traders and quarry lessees - hence the references to 'Merchants' and 'Freemen' - principally for the purpose of transporting stone from the quarries to the shipping piers near Portland Castle. The Portland Railway Co. was granted the requisite Act of Parliament in June 1825 for: '...making and maintaining a railway or tramroad in the Parish of Saint George, in the Isle of Portland....'. An important stipulation of the Act was that the tramway was not to interfere with or impede the military defence of Portland Castle - built during the reign of Henry VIII, it stood on the north side of the 'island' adjacent to where the Admiralty Dockyard was later developed.

The tramway was built to a gauge of 4ft 6in, and started at a point named Priory Corner, some 350ft up on the hill overlooking Fortuneswell. It initially headed in a north-easterly direction, then curved round in horse-shoe fashion, hugging the contour beneath the mighty Verne Citadel to a point near the aptly named Zigzag Road. Thus far, the line was horse worked, having descended by a modest 52ft in one mile - the gradient was with the loads (that is, loaded wagons had the benefit of the downhill grade). From the north side of Zigzag Road the tramway had to descend about 270ft in a distance of 650yds, and this was accomplished with a cable-worked incline. From the foot of the incline the tramway continued, in a horse-worked section, to the shipping pier at Castletown.

The incline, which was on an overall mean gradient of approximately 1 in 7, had two tracks. That said, it should be explained that upper and lower sections of the incline had three rails - the centre rail was 'common' for ascending and descending wagons although, of course,

wagons could not actually pass on those sections. Passing was undertaken at a point midway along the incline, where there were separate up and down tracks. The incline was worked on the 'self acting' principle - a single cable passed from one line of rails to the other, one end of the cable being attached to a descending wagon (loaded) and the other end to a rake of empties. As the loaded wagon descended, the empties at the other end of the rope ascended. At the top of the incline, the cable was wound around a drum (located underground), and this was fitted with a brake so that the speed of the descent could be controlled.

At one time, there was a second incline. This acted as a feeder to the main part of the tramway, connecting with it at a point near the 'horse-shoe' bend beneath Verne Citadel. The course of the second incline can be seen on the accompanying Ordnance Survey maps - it joins the main tramway from the south, almost adjacent to Verne Road crossing. Clearly, it had fallen into disuse and had had its rails lifted by the time the survey was made in 1929.

The tramway opened for business in October 1826. It was authorised to charge the following tonnage rates:
'For all stone of the best quality .... 8d per ton per mile
For all roach stone, capping, ashlars for building, limestone and all other inferior stone .... 6d per ton per mile
For all other goods, commodities, wares and merchandise .... 8d per ton per mile'.

In 1851, a description of the tramway and the method of operations appeared in *Knights Excursion Train Companion* by Charles Knight:
'The block of stone is measured, weighed and marked, and finally lifted on a cart having solid wheels, such as are to be seen in Spain and Morocco. Several horses are yoked to the cart and the stone is dragged to a particular spot, where a tramroad or railway declines to the edge of the sea..... This descending railway is in some parts a remarkable one. It winds round in a circuitous form in order to break the abruptness of the descent, and in certain parts it descends one straight path of uniform declivity by chains and drums. If the block of stone on its cart were allowed to descend at its own speed it would acquire a tremendous velocity before it reached the bottom and would precipitate stone, cart and all into the sea. But there is a chain fastened to the cart at one end and to a string of empty carts at the other, and by being worked over large drums or rollers, the chain pulls up the empty carts while it lowers the filled ones'.

When locomotive-worked railways started to appear on Portland from the 1860s onwards, the 'Merchants Tramway', built to the non-standard gauge of 4ft 6in, could not be physically connected to the other lines. Instead, traffic was physically exchanged at Castleton Sidings*, on the spur from Portland station (Wey-

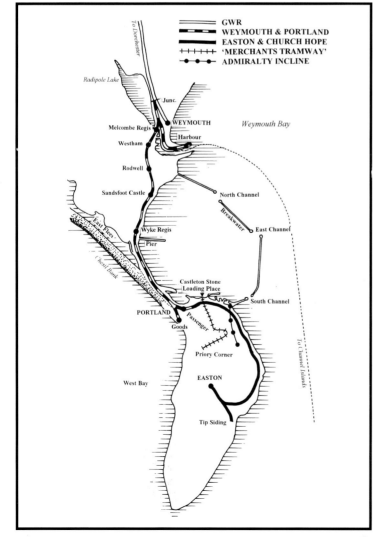

GWR
WEYMOUTH & PORTLAND
EASTON & CHURCH HOPE
'MERCHANTS TRAMWAY'
ADMIRALTY INCLINE

mouth & Portland Railway) which opened in 1865. It looked as if things might change in 1885 when the Easton & Church Hope Railway proposed to take over the tramway and convert it to the 4ft 8½in gauge, but that did not materialise and the tramway was left to carry on as a wholly independent concern.

Despite the tramway's enforced physical isolation, it remained operational until September 1939. As far as can be determined, use had been on the wane for some time before that date, although one of the exchange sidings at Castletown had been lengthened (in an eastward direction) as recently as 1920. The official closure in 1939 came, not as a result of corporate necessity, but as a wartime economy measure. The Portland Railway Company had been operational for almost 123 years - a truly remarkable record. Most of the tramway rails remained in situ until 1957, and although forty years have elapsed since then, the course of the tramway and its inclines can still be easily traced today.

The correct title of the area was Castletown but local railway parlance always referred to Castleton Sidings.

Left. Stone from Bowers Quarry, on the west side of the Isle of Portland, would also have been transported via the Portland Railway prior to 1900. This picture of a vertical boilered steam channeller is particularly interesting as these machines were only rarely used on Portland. These channellers were useful in that they could cut in straight lines - this could be necessary if an excavation had to extend right up to the boundary of a property. The channel cut by the machine can be clearly seen on the right.
PHOTOGRAPH:
BRITISH GEOLOGICAL SURVEY

The 4ft 6in gauge Portland Railway - referred to locally as the 'Merchants Tramway' - descended to Castletown by means of a self-acting incline. As can be seen, the incline had three rails - the centre one being common for ascending and descending wagons - but there was a four-rail passing place half way down. The tramway remained operational until 1939 and the rails weren't lifted until 1957. Note the overbridge near the foot of the incline - this carried the Easton & Church Hope Railway. The lower part of the incline has been redeveloped, but much of the rest, although rather overgrown, can be traced without too much difficulty today.

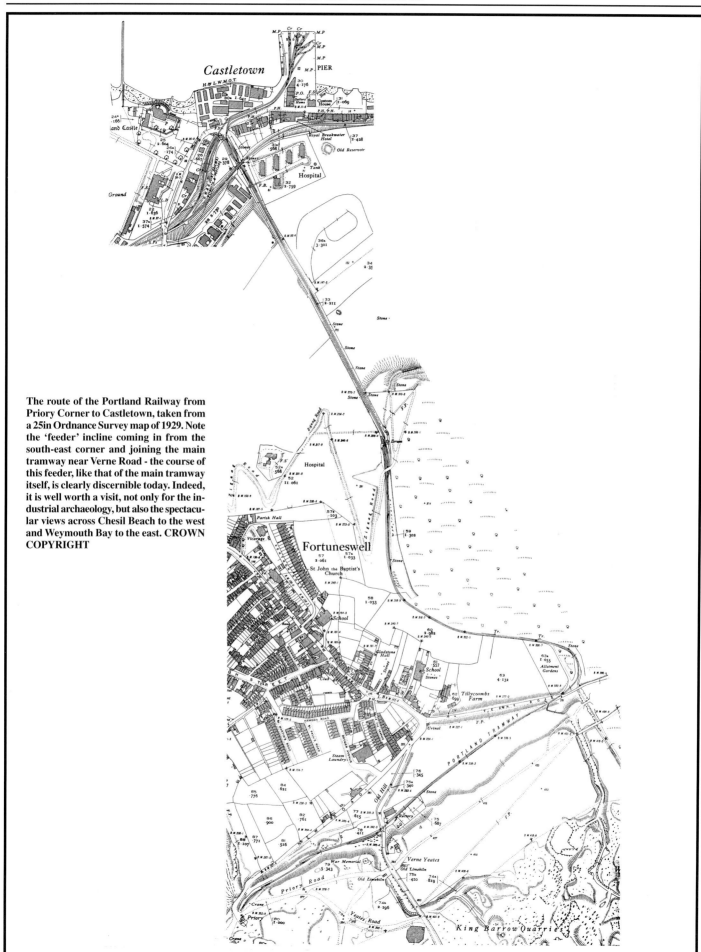

The route of the Portland Railway from Priory Corner to Castletown, taken from a 25in Ordnance Survey map of 1929. Note the 'feeder' incline coming in from the south-east corner and joining the main tramway near Verne Road - the course of this feeder, like that of the main tramway itself, is clearly discernible today. Indeed, it is well worth a visit, not only for the industrial archaeology, but also the spectacular views across Chesil Beach to the west and Weymouth Bay to the east. CROWN COPYRIGHT

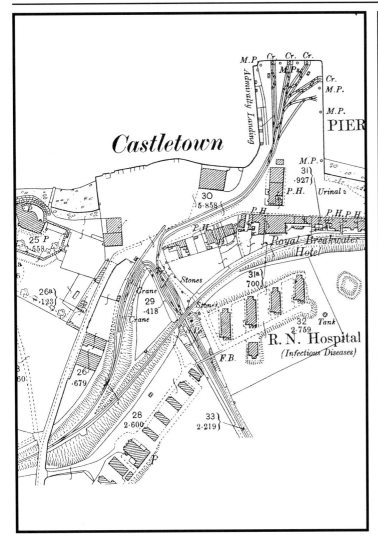

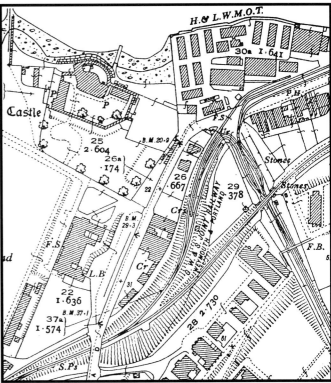

These two Ordnance Survey maps, both taken from 25in originals, show the layout of the exchange facilities at the foot of the Portland Railway incline at two different dates - the incline enters from the bottom right-hand corner. The first map is dated 1903, at which time the Easton & Church Hope Railway (the single line running from bottom left to mid-right of the frame) had only recently opened to passenger traffic. The line bearing in a more northerly direction from the junction is the old Admiralty Line, more of which in Chapter Three...... The second map is dated 1929, and it can be seen that one of the standard gauge exchange sidings has been lengthened. Today, the road overbridge (in the lower left-hand corner) can still be found, as can the foot of the Portland Railway incline, but otherwise, this portion of Portland's railway system has been largely obliterated by Admiralty buildings. CROWN COPYRIGHT

The site of the exchange sidings at Castletown, looking towards HM Dockyard, on 16 January 1965. The Portland Railway ('Merchants Tramway') used to enter from the distance, the incline being out of view on the right - the tramway siding was actually in the 'V' of the two BR lines, beneath the disused gantry crane. At the time this picture was taken the BR lines were nominally in use, but the Merchants Tramway had been out of use for over 25 years. PHOTOGRAPH: COLIN CADDY

Chapter Two

The Weymouth & Portland Railway

After much procrastination, the GWR finally completed the main line to Weymouth on 20 January 1857. This line nominally started at Thingley Junction, just to the west of Chippenham on the London - Bristol main line, and continued via Westbury, Frome, Castle Cary, Yeovil and Dorchester. It had been conceived in 1845 by the Wilts Somerset & Weymouth Railway, but that had fallen on hard times and had been taken over by the GWR. At the time of the take-over only the Wiltshire end of the line had been completed, and so it was left to the GWR to finish the rest. The section of line between Dorchester Junction and Weymouth - just over 6½ miles - was laid with mixed gauge tracks. The broad gauge metals were, of course, for the GWR's own benefit, but the company had been under a legal obligation to provide access for London & South Western Railway trains between Dorchester and Weymouth, hence the additional standard gauge metals.

The arrival of the GWR and LSWR at Weymouth in 1857 triggered thoughts of a branch line from Weymouth to Portland principally, it would seem, as an outlet for Portland stone. The branch line was promoted by the logically-titled Weymouth & Portland Railway Co., but the scheme failed to attract adequate support and was abandoned. However, just five years later a new proposal - using the same corporate title - fared rather better.

On 30 June 1862 the 'new' Weymouth & Portland Railway (W&PR) was formally incorporated to construct a line from Weymouth to the Isle of Portland. The Act also authorised '...an extension of the Wilts Somerset & Weymouth to the Harbour' - this referred to *Weymouth* Harbour (*not* Portland), the extension being in connection with the Channel Island steamer services which had recently been reinstated. It was stipulated that the Portland line was to be laid with mixed gauge rails, rendering it accessible to both GWR and LSWR - indeed, the 'joint' nature of the W&PR actually went a stage further, as the company was leased jointly to the GWR and LSWR.

The Line Completed

The line was ready for the obligatory Board of Trade inspection in the Spring of 1864, Colonel Yolland doing the honours on 20 May. His report began with the customary description of the line: *'....a length of 4 miles 21¾ chains .... laid single throughout, with sidings at Weymouth and Portland, but the land has been purchased and the over-bridges have been constructed to enable a second line to be laid down if hereafter required.* [The provision for future doubling was a common feature of branch line construction in those days, but in the case of the W&PR - as with countless similar lines all over Britain - a second line was never required.] *The width of the line at formation level is 10 feet; it is constructed on the mixed gauge, and the space between the main line and the sidings is 6 feet. It is laid with flat-bottomed rails weighing 62lb per lineal yard, in lengths of 18, 21 and 24 feet.*

No chairs are used as the rails are placed directly on transverse sleepers ..... The rails are secured to the sleepers by two fang bolts through the sleepers near the joints and by fang bolts and screws to the intermediate sleepers. The joints of the rails are fished with a plate on each side .... The sleepers are of Baltic timber, not creosoted. The ballast is partly of broken stone and partly of shingle and sand, said to be 1 foot in depth below the sleepers. There is only one station on the line, which is the terminus at Portland.

'There are 5 under- and 1 over-bridge, besides two viaducts of 489.5 yards [this was the Backwater Viaduct] *and 198 yards* [across the Fleet]. *The underbridges, with one exception, are built of brick or stone .... the greatest span is 21ft 10½ ins. The exception is constructed with wrought iron girders and timber flooring. There are slight evidences of subsidences and movements in the abutments and wing walls of some of these bridges, but nothing of any importance to affect their stability.*

'The viaducts are entirely of wood with openings mostly from 20 to 22 feet, and they are both very unsatisfactory structures. The usual beam for these openings is 2 whole baulks placed one above each other and bolted together - in these viaducts a baulk has been sawn in two parts and then laid one over each other, with bolts through them. The calculated breaking weight of one of these beams is about 11½ tons, but it is very uncertain what weight one of the half baulks would carry. It is quite certain that they are much

Rodwell station opened in 1870, thereby becoming the first intermediate station between Weymouth and Portland. Until 1907 it had only a single platform. This view can be dated between 15 December 1892 (when the signal box opened) and 8 December 1907 (when it was replaced by a brick-built box on the new platform). It is known that, at about this time, Rodwell station had a staff of five; clearly, there was a full turn out for the visit of the photographer. PHOTOGRAPH: JOHN SMITH

The first viaduct across the Backwater at Weymouth was built of timber, and regularly caused consternation to passengers travelling across it. This picture was probably taken only a few years before the viaduct was replaced by a girder structure in 1909. The locomotive is a GWR '2021' class 0-6-0ST (most of the class were later converted to pannier tanks). Even with the aid of a powerful magnifier, the loco cannot be positively identified - it could possibly be No.2040, 2046 or maybe No.2140. Although the train is clearly in motion, this might possibly have been something of a staged shot - given the unusually heavy loading of nine coaches, it could have been some sort of special working. PHOTOGRAPH: R.M. CASSERLEY COLLECTION

too weak, that the workmanship is not good, and from sufficient care not being exercised defective pieces of timber have been made use of. It is very doubtful whether these viaducts will not require to be entirely reconstructed, and it is not clear whether the piles will not give under the weight of an engine. In addition to the strengthening of the beams carrying the load, transoms and through tie rods are required at the centres of the openings.'

The condemnation of the viaducts wasn't the only problem for the Weymouth & Portland Railway. Colonel Yolland also noted:

'1. The railway is unfenced on one side, that next to the sea, for the whole length of the Chesil Beach. This would be unexceptional if the line of low water was in contact with the base of the railway, but this is not the case, as there is a considerable portion of ground bare at low water, including some Common Land belonging to Portland. Persons in boats are in the habit of landing along the Chesil Beach, and although there may not be many cattle, the line should be fenced off so that persons should be kept apart from the line. In one or two other places on the line, the fencing requires attending to.

'2. This railway is to be worked over by the Great Western and the London & South Western Railway Companies, and I understand it is proposed to use the Great Western station at Weymouth. A Joint Committee is to be appointed to regulate the working of the two companies over this line, but that has not yet been done, so that it is uncertain in what manner it is proposed to work the traffic. The junction with the Wilts Somerset & Weymouth [actually, this was now part of the GWR] is made nearly ¼ of a mile north of the Weymouth Station, while on the deposited plans the distance does not exceed 200 yards. Every train arriving at or departing from the Weymouth Station for Portland will therefore require to be shunted over the long distance .... this is an objectionable and dangerous practice.

'3. The signals at the junction with the Wilts Somerset & Weymouth Railway require to be brought together on a properly covered-in stage at the junction; the signals to have the locking apparatus - and a reciprocal ball and arm communication between the Junction Signal Box and the Portland Station.

'4. Some of the sidings leaving the main line at Portland are only constructed for the broad gauge, and others only for the narrow. In all cases the mixed gauge should be completed to avoid danger by the presentation of the narrow gauge facing points to a broad gauge train, and the converse.

'5. Adequate accommodation is not provided at Portland Station for two companies to work traffic independently of each other. It is quite possible that enough has been done to enable one Company to work the local traffic between Portland and Weymouth, but the Great

Western and London & South Western Railway Companies will probably both propose to work their regular trains, and also excursion trains on to Portland within a short interval of time from each other. A covered platform for each company will eventually be required of a greater length than the existing platform, and also additional sidings for the reception of carriages etc. [Separate facilities for the GWR and LSWR at Portland were never provided.] If, however, it is intended by these Companies to make Portland their Terminal Station in stead of Weymouth it is very questionable whether they should not bear a portion if not the whole of the cost of adapting this Station for a Terminal Station - and in that case an Engine Turntable would be required. [Colonel Yolland seemed to be taking into account the possibility of friction between the GWR and the LSWR - such caution was

Crossing the Chesil causeway - on 14 July 1951, O2 No.30223 heads for Ferrybridge with a train for Weymouth. Given the angle of the sun, this could possibly be the 5.19pm ex-Easton which was due at Melcombe Regis at 5.46pm. In the far distance on the left of the locomotive, the prison stands on top of the rocky outcrop. At the time of writing, another prison (a ship) has just arrived at Portland - it will, presumably, be equally impracticable for inmates to tunnel their way out of. PHOTOGRAPH: R.H. TUNSTALL

Scheduled passenger services ceased on the Portland branch in 1952, but the line remained open for goods traffic until 1965. In Autumn 1963 Ivatt 2-6-2Ts had taken over the goods workings from the WR pannier tanks; this is No.41305 on the Chesil with a Weymouth - Portland goods on 14 September 1963. The locomotive had been transferred from Eastleigh to Weymouth in June, and still sported the 71A shed plate of its former home. PHOTOGRAPH: COLIN CADDY

sensible, as in several areas the two companies had already become rather unneighbourly neighbours.]

'6. One fang bolt at least should be used for securing each rail to the intermediate sleepers - and two on the sleeper in the middle of the rails length. In some instances, at present, only a screw is used.'

Clearly, Colonel Yolland was far from satisfied with the works and arrangements, and it came as little surprise that he declined to sanction the opening of the railway. One of the causes of dissatisfaction had been the viaducts, and these were given prompt attention. The structures were remodelled and strengthened as regards the longitudinal timbers, and additional piles were also driven in. Nevertheless, when Colonel Yolland reinspected the line on 6 August 1864 he was unimpressed by the condition of the railway on the viaducts, noting that '....the ballast of shingle and fine sand does not enable

the packing of the sleepers to be well done, and the fine sand will fall gradually through the planking and either some chalk should be added or the rails be laid on longitudinal instead of cross-sleepers.'

But that was, in effect, the good news. There was ample bad news - elsewhere along the line, the fencing, signalling and fitting of additional fang bolts had still not been completed, and the arrangements at Weymouth station were still unresolved. Furthermore, as the GWR and LSWR had not yet determined how they were to work the traffic on the W&PR, Colonel Yolland stipulated that a turntable be installed at Portland, principally for turning the engines of excursion trains. This, however, was never provided.

Problems at Weymouth

Mention was made of the arrangements at Weymouth being unsatisfactory. A glance at one of the accompanying maps will show that the Portland line joined the main line about 600 yards north of Weymouth station - this was part of the overall problem. The railway company proposed that branch trains should be reversed between the junction and the station, and in view of the potential hazards, the Board of Trade would have none of it: '....there is no

instance on record of the Board of Trade having sanctioned the opening of a new line of railway where every passenger train that arrives or departs from one of the Terminal Stations must be backed one-third of a mile .... nothing will induce the Board of Trade to sanction this .... bad accidents have arisen [elsewhere] from the shunting of trains in the dark, through station yards which are generally in much worse state of repair than the other portions of the line, and through points and crossings'. There was also the matter of locos fouling the main line at the station while running round their trains.

In order to avoid the hazards of reversing, the BoT stipulated that, unless Weymouth station were to be completely remodelled (a somewhat impractical suggestion!), Portland trains should be hauled loco-first between the junction and the station - in other words the loco would have to run round its train at the junction. Of necessity, this procedure was subsequently adopted, but it was a positive hindrance to the smooth operation of Portland branch trains - and extremely unpopular with the travelling public - for many years to come.

The problem of entry to and exit from Weymouth station having been resolved, after a fashion, and other deficiencies rectified to the satisfaction of the Board of Trade, it seemed that the Portland line was finally ready for opening. But it was not so, for there was another major problem at Weymouth. No designated accommodation had been made for Portland trains - the W&PR claimed that the provision of facilities was the responsibility of the LSWR, but the LSWR didn't share that opinion. Indeed, the LSWR contended that, if necessary, the W&PR should construct a separate station where branch trains could terminate close to the main line station. While the dispute remained unresolved, the absence of the necessary facilities at Weymouth meant that, even after all this time, the line still could not be opened to public traffic.

In November 1864 it seemed that a solution to the dispute might be on the horizon as, at the request of the W&PR and LSWR, an arbitrator was appointed by the Board of Trade. The W&PR hoped that this would soon '....put an end to the scandal of this property remaining so long unproductive', but an early settlement was not on the cards. This was largely due to the GWR's entry into the dispute - as the actual owner of Weymouth station, it was not surprising that it wanted a say, if only to ensure that its own interests were not compromised. Indeed, part of the LSWR defence in the dispute had been to blame the GWR for having requested an unreasonably high sum to accommodate W&PR trains! This helped the little W&PR not one whit, and to add insult to injury the company had to pay contractors for keeping the line in good order - traffic or no traffic.

The matter dragged on into the spring of 1865, when the arbitrator's decision was finally announced. The decision went in favour of the 'big boys' - it was considered that, as an independent concern and despite the working agreement, the Weymouth & Portland Railway was liable to provide station facilities at the Weymouth end of its line. If the W&PR services were to use the main line station at Weymouth, pay-

> THE DANGEROUS LEVEL-CROSSING AT THE BACK-WATER BRIDGE.—Mr. HURDLE proposed that the attention of the Weymouth and Portland Railway Company be again drawn to the dangerous nature of the level-crossing on the western side of the Backwater bridge, and that they be called upon either to provide a proper foot-bridge or to set back the two wicket gates so that the two footpaths on both sides may be properly completed." Mr. Hurdle laid stress on the dangerous nature of the pair of wicket gates, for the man upstairs working the points could not see below who was standing between the gates. When the gates were put there there were not 200 people living in Westham (Mr. GROVES: Not more than 20.) Now there were nearly 4,000 people living in the Westham district and passing daily time after time. The vehicular traffic had also increased in proportion, yet the gate remained of the same width. Mr. FROOM seconded the motion, and it was carried unanimously.

A local press report on a meeting of the Weymouth Town Council, 2 May 1900.

ment for the use of the main line station was the responsibility of the W&PR itself. But even this landmark decision did not herald the immediate opening of the line, as the three railway companies quibbled about the precise terms of the arrangements.

Open At Last

The Weymouth - Portland line finally opened to traffic in October 1865 - more than a year since the railway had been 'passed' as satisfactory. There seems to have been a ceremonial opening on 9 October (and it is possible that goods trains were accommodated from this date) but it was Monday 16 October before public passenger services commenced. The first train was the 7.30am from Weymouth to Portland, which comprised six four-wheeled coaches hauled by Beattie 2-4-0WT No.154 NILE - in the words of the local newspaper, the *Weymouth Telegraph*, the train conveyed '....the first freight of living souls to Portland'. The newspaper pointed out - somewhat bizarrely, perhaps - that the railway would be of particular use '...*In case of anything happening to disturb the peace and har-*

mony which happily prevail [on Portland] *troops can be conveyed from Portsmouth or elsewhere in a very short time....'* On a marginally less alarmist note, it added that: '....*should an outbreak ever take place among the convicts* [of Portland Prison] *the military from Weymouth would be so quickly at hand that any attempt at insubordination must be speedily crushed'.*

As far as can be determined, the original arrangement was that the LSWR should work the passenger services and its own goods services - on the standard gauge, of course - while the GWR worked its own goods trains on the broad gauge. It is believed that there was *never* a scheduled broad gauge passenger working on the line. Theoretically or otherwise, the scope for broad gauge workings ceased completely on 18 June 1874 when broad gauge operations came to an end, not only on the Portland branch, but also on the entire length of the GWR main line between Thingley Junction and Weymouth, the old Wilts Somerset & Weymouth. Following the 'narrowing' of the Portland branch, the usual pattern was for the GWR and LSWR to work the passenger traffic on alternate years.

For the next fifteen years or so the W&PR's existence was relatively uneventful, save for the opening of an intermediate station at Rodwell in 1870 and - on a gloomier note - three separate accidents at Portland station. The first was on 13 September 1876 - the brakes of an incoming train failed, and it collided with empty stock at the station platform. Several passengers were injured, some seriously. At the ensuing enquiry the Board of Trade wasted no time in championing the use of continuous brakes.

Fay's brakes were duly fitted to the branch passenger train (there seems to have been, at that time, a designated branch set), but an accident at Portland on Sunday 23 December 1877 was again blamed (at first) on the brakes having failed. On this occasion, the 9.30am GWR passenger train from Weymouth to Portland collided with an empty coach standing in the arrival bay at the terminus, with eight passengers 'slightly injured'. The train comprised seven vehicles in the following order:
1) first and second class composite
2) first class
3) third class brake
4) third class
5) third class
6) second class
7) third class brake

The last five of these were fitted with continuous brakes. The train crew claimed that the brakes had failed, but there was more than a hint of conspiracy. The day after the accident, a ganger had 'happened to find' a cast iron bracket (part of the brake apparatus) on the line about $1\frac{1}{2}$ miles north of Portland station. Wasn't the shearing of this bracket the cause of the brake failure? Not so, it seemed. When the inspecting officer had tested the brakes after the accident he had found them to be in working order - conspicuously, this was *without* the bracket in question. The inspector was reliably informed that the bracket could only have come adrift as a result of the actual collision, and he opined that the sheared bracket: '....*must have been carried to the point $1\frac{1}{2}$ miles from the station for the purpose of supporting the statement that the continuous breaks had become defective...'.* The inspector's report concluded that the accident had had nothing to do with a brake failure, but had been due to the train being driven at too high a speed on the approach to Portland station. As for his suspicions concerning the 'missing' bracket, nothing could be proved.....

Another accident occurred on 6 November 1892, this time near Backwater Viaduct. The 4.00pm Portland - Weymouth passenger train,

The Victoria Square end of the much-unloved W&P passenger terminus at Portland. As related later in the book, following the construction of a new station on an adjacent site in 1905 the original terminus became a goods station. This picture was taken on 6 February 1965, only a couple of months before the line closed completely. **PHOTOGRAPH: COLIN CADDY**

Weymouth, taken from a 25in Ordnance Survey map. Although this survey was made in 1929 and shows Melcombe Regis station (which opened in 1909, principally to circumvent the problems of reversal at Weymouth), the nature of the problems can be clearly seen. The branch comes in from the south west, and prior to 1909 trains had to cross the neck of the goods yard and the main running lines, then change direction (with the loco running round to the other end of the train) in order to reach the terminus. This arrangement was riddled with dangers...CROWN COPYRIGHT.

Portland Terminus

By the early 1890s, certain local businessmen and community leaders had become very dissatisfied with the facilities at Portland station and the manner in which the branch line was worked. The principal causes of unrest were voiced on 7 January 1891 by Mr. Henry Sansom for the Portland Local Board (the formal title of the local administrative body at that time) in a petition to the GWR and LSWR: '....owing to the increase of the Goods and Passenger traffic to Portland, and to the growing importance of the Island, the present arrangements for Railway Communication between it and London and other places are quite insufficient and greater facilities for the same are required .... further, the present Station accommodation at Portland is unsatisfactory and deficient, in consequence of which the use of the Station is often attended with inconvenience and danger to the Public'.

Other petitions citing similar grievances followed, and on 18 December 1891 Mr. Edward Pearce (also of the Portland Local Board) urged the Board of Trade to intervene, with special regard to: '....the dangerous shunting on the Portland Railway at Weymouth [this referred to the 'running round' at the junction - a procedure demanded by the Board of Trade due to the layout of the junction] and the condition of the wooden railway bridge over the Backwater there....also the insufficient facilities for loading and unloading at the Traffic Depot at Portland, whereby much hindrance and loss of time is occasioned....' Captain Fellowes of the HMS ALEXANDRA was also quick to criticise the state of the line and the level of the services. (HMS ALEXANDRA, incidentally, was commissioned in 1875 as a destroyer, but from 1891 to 1901 was used as a coastguard base at 'Weymouth'. She was taken out of service in 1908).

Not altogether unexpectedly, the petitions didn't prod the GWR and LSWR into immediate action. In their joint response dated 25 February 1892, the companies countered that, with regard to connections with London trains at Weymouth: '....there are between Portland and London 4 down trains and 4 up trains by the Great Western route and 6 down and 6 up by the South Western Route, which having regard to the limited traffic passing between the points in question, amply meet the requirements'. This response was factually correct, but with the first departure from Portland being at 7.45am, the first available London connection at Weymouth was the 8.35am (which took five hours to Waterloo) - and that assumed that the branch train arrived on time, which was not always the case. It was not particularly convenient for business travellers. Regarding the station accommodation at Portland, the GWR and LSWR pointed out that: '....in February of last year the companies incurred the expense of extending the platform by 100 feet, and it is now sufficiently long to hold 11 carriages, which meets the ordinary requirements.'

But the local railway-using public were far from satisfied. By the mid-1890s the level of services, the facilities and the general state of the railway were attracting increasingly vociferous criticism. The local authorities opined that matters had become even more acute because

hauled by LSWR O2 0-4-4T No.180 (which finished life on the Isle of Wight in March 1967 as W31 CHALE), partially derailed near the north end of the viaduct, the left-hand wheels of the locomotive and five of the six carriages dropping inside the left-hand rail. Fortunately, the train remained upright and nobody was injured. It was found that some of the rail fastenings had given way, but there was no obvious explana-

tion for this. It was suggested that the superelevation of the outer rail on the viaduct (superelevation was required as the viaduct was on a 23-chain curve) might possibly be a little higher than was necessary. This would increase the pressure on the inside of the lower rail, but the reporting officer conceded that this, alone, was most unlikely to have been the cause of the accident.

of the huge growth in traffic - the figures quoted were:

Passengers (single journeys): *1890 - 94,214; 1895 - 259,734; 1896 - 291,349; increase over six years - 197,135 (309%)*

Goods and minerals (tons): *1890 - 31,182; 1895 - 44,112; 1896 - 56,528; increase over six years - 25,346 (81.3%)*

Livestock (wagons): *1890 - n/a; 1895 - 142; 1896 - 238; increase over ONE year - 96 (67.6%)*

During the late 1890s the traffic continued to increase (by 1898 the population of the Isle of Portland was stated to be just over 10,000) and this of course made a bad situation even worse. Following yet another bout of criticism, on 28 September 1898 the GWR explained to the Portland Local Board that, during the previous six years not only had Portland station been extended, but it had been provided with a new covering ('a botch of a covering' according to one regular passenger). Moreover, the sidings, yard, cranes, as well as the locking and signalling had been 'altered', a lamp room converted into a cloak room, and 'additional W.C. and Urinal' accommodation provided. The GWR also pointed out that an extra Saturday evening train which had been introduced for the summer of 1893 was now a year-round feature of the timetables; in the company's opinion the existing level of service (nine trains each way plus the 'Saturday Special') was 'fair and reasonable'.

However, this did not satisfy the complainants. Dorset's local newspaper, the *County Times,* added its weight to the controversy on 17 December 1898, its leader referring to the: '....scandalous state of things which the public have had for years to endure on the Portland railway, and especially at the terminal station'. The railway was described as: '....the Cinderella among local lines...' and it was stated that: '....the scenes which are to be witnessed almost daily and nightly at Portland Station are a disgrace. The narrow exposed platform is a positive death trap, and if some day there is a loss of life it will be a ghastly fulfilment of the predictions that have so often been expressed....'. As for the joint operation of the railway, the newspaper considered that: '.....divided interests operate with a most disastrous result so far as the public are concerned....', and urged local people to '....reject the soothing syrup recently administered by the railway companies'.

The newspaper urged locals to petition the Board of Trade to take action, and the local council itself (in the person of Mr. Merrick Head) duly wrote to the BoT on 28 December 1898: '....*the sidings at Portland Station are so much blocked through the excess of goods traffic, that the Passengers Platform is constantly used for the unloading of Cat-*

tle, Sheep, gear of War and other materials. The narrow platform is often so crowded that it is difficult to move along it or to pass out of the Station, and passengers are in imminent danger of being crowded on to the line of rails on either side of it.....' It did not go down too well that, while the passengers' complaints seemed to be fobbed off, extra goods trains had been put on and the goods staff at Portland had almost doubled in number.

There was another newspaper broadside, on this occasion from the *Southern Times* on 7 January 1899. The salvo referred to the previous Monday, 2 January: *'The 7.30am train into Portland arrived at 8.05am, hence the 7.35am train from Portland started at 8.17am. The unfortunate passengers were kept shivering in the booking office and on the platform for three-quarters of an hour. In the bad-smelling waiting room no attempt was made to light a fire until after 7.30..... At Weymouth we expected the usual shunting, when a strange thing happened. The Railway Company really had a pilot engine, which they fastened to the other end of the train and brought it into the siding without any shunting. The only explanation that could be given was that it was the new year and the company had been forming a good resolution. This actually turned out to be the fact, for, like all good resolutions, it was made to be broken. The old shunting went on again when the train returned to Portland'.* The report continued by quoting specific instances of passengers who had been thoroughly inconvenienced by the poor timekeeping and the consequent missing of connections.

The potential dangers of the shunting arrangements at Weymouth were brought home on 10 April 1899 when someone was knocked down and killed by a train at the Weston Esplanade level crossing (adjacent to the point where the Portland branch joined the main line - near to what is now the junction of Radipole Park Drive and King Street). This was not the first

such accident at that point. At the inquest, it was remarked that pedestrians often had their view of the railway obstructed by wagons standing in the sidings, and the practice of branch engines running round trains at this point made matters even more hazardous.

However, when faced with criticism of the reversals and running-round at Weymouth, the GWR and LSWR had the heaven-sent excuse that those practices had, in fact, been at the insistence of the Board of Trade. Moreover, the railway companies could claim - with a degree of justification - that a proposed safety measure for pedestrians had effectively been vetoed by the Weymouth Corporation. That safety measure had taken the form of a footbridge over the line - after a fatal accident in 1865 the railway companies had offered to provide a footbridge with steps, but had requested that the Corporation pay the difference in cost if '....a bridge with ramps for the accommodation of bath chairs is required'. The Corporation had actually objected to the footbridge. Following the fatality of 1899, it was agreed to install an alarm bell at the level crossing.

Another aspect of the manoeuvres at Weymouth was that they were time consuming. Indeed, it was estimated that each manoeuvre took at least five minutes - and that assumed no holdups caused by other movements at the station. It was alleged that 'more than half' of the passengers travelling between Weymouth and Portland preferred to alight at Rodwell (where there were no facilities at that time - not even a shelter) and walk to or from the town centre, rather than 'submit to the insufferable delay in shunting at Weymouth'. It is, however, difficult to prove or disprove that claim.

Matters weren't resolved for some time - indeed, some of the sources of discontent were *never* properly addressed. The problems at Portland station and the controversial shunting arrangements at Weymouth were, however, side-stepped, more of which anon...

It is believed that the train headed by 517 class 0-4-2T No.215 at Platform 3 of Weymouth station is for the Portland Branch. We have an interesting glimpse of the station signal box which remained operational until 1957. PHOTOGRAPH: J. SMITH

Chapter Three
The Admiralty Line

In 1794 the Admiralty was urged to construct a breakwater at Portland in order to provide a safe anchorage for Naval vessels. At that time, Britain considered France to be the threat, and it was felt that an additional anchorage on the south coast would be a sensible precaution against an anticipated blockade of the English Channel. However, the idea for the Portland breakwater was held in abeyance and did not arise again until 1846. This time, there was a far more positive tone, and in 1847 an Act of Parliament was obtained for the construction of a 1½-mile long breakwater.

The construction work commenced in August 1847, but because much of the initial work was of a preliminary nature it was 25 July 1849 before the foundation stone was ceremonially laid, by Albert, the Prince Consort. Anything from 600 to 1,000 convicts were employed on the work at any one time, and others were put to work in the local quarries, from where the stone was extracted. A prison was built at The Grove (380ft up on the hill overlooking the site) to accommodate up to 1,300 convicts.

The breakwater consumed a vast amount of stone - ultimately around six million tons - some of which was extracted at Grove Quarries near the prison, 380ft up on the hill overlooking the site. The stone from these quarries was brought down to the construction site by means of a cable-worked incline; known, somewhat logically, as the Admiralty Incline, its foot was

almost adjacent to the landward end of the breakwater itself.

The construction of the breakwater was a massive exercise, and befitting a project of such a scale, the contractor - J.T. Leather (later the owner of the famous Hunslet Engine Co. of Leeds) - installed a railway on the site. Remarkably for such a railway, it was built to a gauge of 7ft 0¼in; this was, of course, the precise measurement of the GWR's broad gauge, but this could not have been with regard to outside connections, as the contractor's line is known to have been in operation by about 1852 - thirteen years before the mixed gauge Weymouth & Portland line opened.

On, or shortly after, the opening of the Weymouth & Portland line in October 1865, a ¼-mile long siding was installed from Portland terminus to Castletown. The siding's principal purpose was to enable stone to be transhipped from the foot of the old 'Merchants Tramway' (q.v.), but given that the breakwater construction site was only about ¾-mile beyond Castletown it is, perhaps, surprising that the branch line was not extended to the construction site, as it would have offered a potentially useful route for construction traffic.

After twenty-three years of construction work, Portland breakwater was finally completed in 1872, the last stone being ceremonially laid by the Prince Consort on 10 August. (That date was quoted in *The Times* - some other sources have since quoted 18 August). The Admiralty required rail access to the breakwater, principally to bring in coal for the ships, and so it was proposed to construct a railway, a little over a mile in length, from the Portland & Weymouth line to the breakwater. Somewhat conveniently, it would seem, the Portland end of the proposed line would

be formed by a section of the existing Castletown siding.

Under an agreement of May 1874 the GWR and LSWR would jointly construct and work the Admiralty Line - or the Portland Breakwater Railway, as it was alternatively known - but with the cost of the works and the working expenses being paid by the Admiralty. The line was formally authorised by an LSWR Act of July 1875 and was completed in May 1877, but due largely to recurring landslips it could not open to traffic until 1878. Despite the GWR's and LSWR's involvement with the line, it was horse worked. That said, a note of caution is in order - most sources refer *exclusively* to horse-working, but a letter from the Admiralty to the Board of Trade in 1900 refers to the line being worked '....*principally* by horses'. Whatever the case, traffic over the Admiralty Line was of a very light nature. That, however, changed in 1900 when the Easton & Church Hope Railway opened to goods traffic, exercising its running powers over the Admiralty Line. By 1902 the line had been satisfactorily upgraded to permit the introduction of public passenger services.....but more of this anon.

..........oOo..........

As for the Admiralty presence at Portland, the dockyard became one of Britain's major Naval bases, and was continually expanded for the best part of a century. The dockyard was ultimately served by a substantial internal railway system which converted to locomotive traction *circa* 1900. The first locomotives were purchased from the contractor engaged on the construction of the breakwater extensions. Over the years, seven steam and two diesel locomotives were used at the dockyard, though not all simultaneously. The steam locos were all outside cylinder 0-4-0STs - four Bagnalls, two Pecketts and one Barclay - while the diesels were Fowler 0-4-0s. The dockyard remained rail-connected until the closure of the Weymouth - Portland - Easton branch line in 1965, and it is thought that there might have been some internal rail traffic for another year or so. The last locomotives - the two diesels - went for scrap in 1967.

Above. **Castletown Junction, 16 January 1965. The original W&P branch to the exchange sidings veers off right, while the Admiralty Line continues left - the junction almost underneath the bridge actually marked the 'zero' point of the Admiralty Line . PHOTOGRAPH: COLIN CADDY**

Below. **Hospital halt was just 175 yards along the line from Castletown Junction. The halt was for the private use of the Navy, the R.N. hospital being almost adjacent - the roof of the first block can be seen above the shrubbery on the right. The iron bridge seen at the far end of the platform carries the line over the foot of the Portland Railway incline. CROWN COPYRIGHT**

Above. Easton station, the terminus of the line for passengers, probably in the period 1905-10. The station building had been largely reconstructed following a fire of 1903. The engine shed, seen on the left, opened in 1905. The bridge at the far end of the station carries Reforne Street over the railway. The 1909 Swindon allocation register reveals that 2021 class 0-6-0STs Nos.2038 and 2044 took turns outstationed at Easton during the year. At this period, Easton station had a staff of 6 or 7, but only four pose for the camera. PHOTOGRAPH: J. SMITH

Below. Easton station, looking from Reforne Street bridge, probably in the 1930s. The footbridge in the distance carried a footpath between Bloomfield Terrace and Railway Road - it was not accessible from the station. O2 0-4-4T No.193 (later BR No.30193) prepares to run round its four-coach train. PHOTOGRAPH: J. SMITH

Chapter Four
The Easton & Church Hope Railway

The Easton & Church Hope Railway (E&CHR) was incorporated on 25 July 1867 to construct: '....a railway from Easton, in the Isle of Portland, to Church Hope Cove*, with a pier in connection therewith. Length 1½ miles.' The railway was intended to provide an alternative outlet for stone from the quarries in and around Easton. The plans had to allow for the fact that Easton was some 300ft above sea level, and so the proposed route involved two reversals - a sort of zigzag - and also a 1 in 8 cable-worked incline. Quite remarkably, the plans seem to have been for a broad gauge line. If the intention had been for the E&CHR to connect with the Weymouth & Portland Railway the use of the broad gauge - to facilitate through traffic - would have made sense; however, since the proposed E&CHR was an isolated line, the use of the broad gauge was not only odd but, given the nature of the line, thoroughly eccentric.

Only part of the proposed line - a ¾-mile long section from Easton to Southwell Road - was constructed before the powers lapsed in 1872. As far as can be determined, this completed portion of the line never accommodated any revenue-earning traffic - at least, not for almost thirty years. To get even this far, the E&CHR had had to fork out almost £22,000 - £10,700 for engineering and works, £3,500 for legal expenses and almost £7,600 for purchase of land and compensation, although it should be emphasised that the sum for 'purchase of land' seems to have included the land for the unbuilt portion of the railway.

*(*Despite the title of the railway company being the Easton & Church **Hope** Railway, the correct title for the local landmark was Church **Ope** Cove. Nevertheless, in many railway company documents the landmark was incorrectly spelt).*

Reincarnation
The project lay dormant until the early 1880s, when thoughts turned to reviving the uncompleted E&CHR. The company was still extant - and was still incurring administrative charges of around £17 per annum! - so a new scheme was promoted under the same corporate identity. This involved the formal abandonment of the unfinished section to Church Ope Cove, and the construction, instead, of an extension to the Admiralty Line (q.v.), over which running powers would be exercised in order to connect with the Weymouth & Portland line. The new works were authorised in August 1884. These works encompassed 3¼ miles of new railways including, not only the extension towards Portland, but also a short branch from Easton (near Pennsylvania Road) to Weston.

Revised powers were granted in August 1887 - these included an alternative alignment for the Weston branch, and also an extension northwards from Easton to connect with the old horse-worked Portland Railway near Priory Corner. Construction finally commenced in 1888, but this did not trigger the start of an all-out endeavour - the powers for the Weston branch and the extension to Priory Corner were left to lapse, and there were no less that five extensions of time before the line even looked like coming to fruition. If nothing else, the E&CHR did not have to address any problems of gauges, as broad gauge workings on Portland had ceased in June 1874.

On 5 August 1897 the E&CHR entered an agreement for its lines to be worked jointly by the GWR and LSWR, at a rate of 2/6d per train mile. It was calculated that the cost of working six passenger trains and one goods each way daily would be £4,132 per annum, but the local company estimated that the traffic would generate revenue of over £13,000 per annum, almost two-thirds of which would be accounted for by goods and mineral traffic.

It might be considered that the ratification of a working agreement heralded the imminent opening of the line, but not so. Over three years were to elapse before the line was ready for traffic. The delay was partly attributable to the need for considerable improvements to the Admiralty Line, over which the E&CHR was to exercise running powers. Among the necessary improvements was the reconstruction of a retaining wall on the Admiralty Line near Castletown, an increase in the headway from 9ft to 14ft under the old Portland Railway incline, and general upgrading to permit locomotive haulage.

Unfortunately for the E&CHR, in 1899 the Admiralty purchased its section of line outright from the GWR and LSWR for a sum of £20,909.1s.0d - half to each company. (It had previously paid an annuity equal to 4%.) The Admiralty, as sole proprietors, made it quite

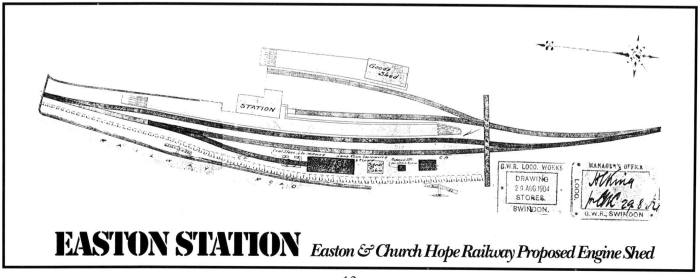

EASTON STATION *Easton & Church Hope Railway Proposed Engine Shed*

Quarry Tip siding, which formed part of the original (uncompleted) E&CHR, is seldom, if ever, seen in photographs. A block of stone is being loaded into a wagon belonging to the United Stone Firms - the wagon half hidden on the right seems to be lettered L M S. The building in the distance on the left is Pennsylvania Castle. The date is April 1930. PHOTOGRAPH: BRITISH GEOLOGICAL SURVEY

clear that the costs for bringing the line up to passenger-carrying standards would have to be borne wholly by the E&CHR, but there was no suggestion that the E&CHR would be granted a reduction in the agreed charge for the use of the line (£900 p.a.). The E&CHR was not altogether amused by this turn of affairs.

The E&CHR therefore had to pay for the necessary improvements itself, but it was August 1901 before the company obtained authorisation to carry out the works. In the meantime - on 31 May 1900 - Colonel Yorke inspected the E&CHR from the junction with the Admiralty Line to the terminus at Easton. He noted ominously that the line '....differed materially to that shewn in any of the plans....', but this was hardly surprising as some of those plans had been drawn up 33 years earlier.

The inspection report began with the customary description: '... *3 miles 39½ chains in length .... gauge is 4' 8½" and is single through-*

The Bath & Portland Stone Firms were served by their own private siding - Bottomcombe Siding - as from 17 April 1924. This was part of a major modernisation programme of the stone works, another aspect being the provision of an electrically-operated overhead crane; as the plaque denotes, the crane was built by Sir William Arrol of Glasgow in 1925 and had a capacity of 5 tons. Note the railway wagons of the GWR, SR, LMS and LNER (this one with a separate 'piggy-back' container) - the local stone was clearly set for destinations far and wide. This fine picture was taken in April 1930. PHOTOGRAPH: BRITISH GEOLOGICAL SURVEY

Inside the Bath & Portland Co. workshop at Easton, April 1930. PHOTOGRAPH: BRITISH GEOLOGICAL SURVEY

out .... steepest gradient 1 in 40, sharpest curve 15 chains .... most important cutting has a maximum depth of 58ft and the highest embankment a height of 29ft .... bull-headed steel rails 76lb to the yard .... ballast of broken Portland stone .... four bridges and one viaduct under and six bridges over the line; two of the underbridges and the viaduct are constructed with steel girders resting on stone piers and abutments, the other two, which are small, consisting of corrugated steel troughing on stone abutments...'

Easton station was described as having: *'....a simple platform 300ft long, a loop line for enabling engines to run round, and a goods yard and sidings. The station buildings comprise a booking hall and general waiting room, a ladies room and lavatory accommodation for both sexes'.* It was noted that: *'....the line at the north end of the station is continued as a mineral line to some quarries, and safety catch points are provided on the mineral line to protect trains in the station from wagons which may break loose*

from the quarries.' There was, however, a note of caution about the arrangements to the south of Easton station: *'The line which joins the main line at Quarry Tip Junction* [i.e. the spur to Southwell Road which formed part of the 'original' E&CHR of 1867] *is at present to be used as a mineral line only .... this railway crosses the public road from Easton to Church Hope* [sic] *on the level .... gates and a gatekeeper's lodge should be provided at this crossing, and owing to the gradient, catch points should be provided on the upper side of the crossing to intercept*

An uncluttered view of Easton station, said to be about 1905. If that date is correct, the engine shed would have been virtually new. PHOTOGRAPH: R.M. CASSERLEY COLLECTION

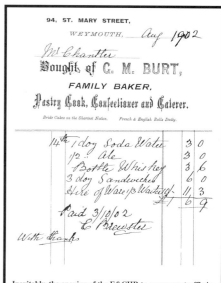

94, ST. MARY STREET,

WEYMOUTH, *Aug 1902*

Mr Chantler

Bought of C. M. BURT,

FAMILY BAKER,

Pastry Cook, Confectioner and Caterer.

Bride Cakes on the Shortest Notice.   French & English Rolls Daily.

14th 1 doz Soda Water	3	0
1/2 Ale	3	0
Bottle Whiskey	3	6
3 doz Sandwiches	6	0
Hire of Ware 1/3 Waiting	11	3
	£1 6	9

Paid 3/10/02
E Brewster
With thanks

Inevitably, the opening of the E&CHR to passenger traffic in August 1902 warranted some sort of beanfeast, although '...one dozen soda water, half dozen ale, 3 doz. sandwiches etc....' doesn't exactly suggest a binge for all and sundry. This invoice was made out to the L&SWR's agent, Mr. Chantler.

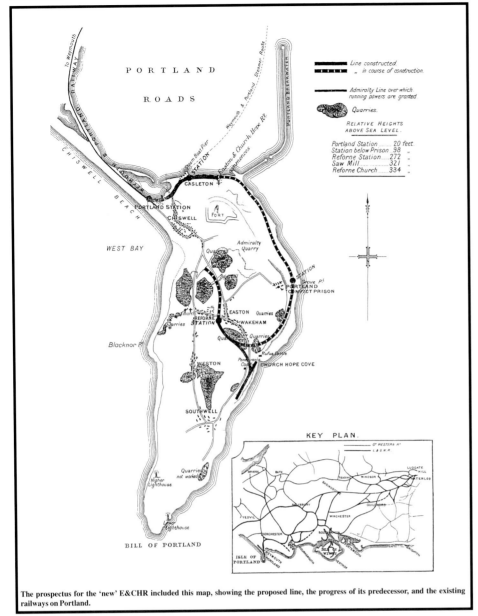

The prospectus for the 'new' E&CHR included this map, showing the proposed line, the progress of its predecessor, and the existing railways on Portland.

vehicles which might break loose from the siding.'

As for signalling, it was reported that: 'The only signals on the line are those at Easton station. The signal box here, from which the siding connections, loop points and signals are worked, contains 11 levers in use and 3 spare'. Colonel Yorke noted certain requirements regarding the interlocking of signals at Easton, but was otherwise satisfied with this aspect. (The points controlling the Quarry Tip siding and also those at the Admiralty end of the line were each worked from a 2-lever ground frame, locked by a key on the train staff).

In the absence of a turntable at Easton, it was stipulated that the line be worked: '....by tank engines only, which should be fitted with sand pipes and brake pipes at both ends, and to be suitable in all respects for running bunker in front, care being taken that the coal carried in the bunker shall not obscure the view of the line and signals etc. from the driver...'

In all, Colonel Yorke was generally satisfied with the railway, but could not recommend that it be opened to passenger traffic. The problem was that, at the northern end of the line, E&CHR had nowhere to go. The E&CHR actually connected with the Admiralty Line (over which running powers were to be exercised to Portland station) but the Admiralty Line was still far from ready to accommodate passenger traffic. The principal aspects requiring attention were: '....an underbridge of insufficient strength and a retaining wall of doubtful stability, and an absence of proper signalling arrangements....'

Technically, the E&CHR could have opened to goods traffic *without* having been 'passed' by the Board of Trade, whose approval was required only for public passenger traffic. This troubled Mr. Merrick Head of the Portland Local Board. Mr. Head declared: '....the lives of Railway Officials, Engine Drivers, Guardsmen and other employees are as much entitled to be protected as ordinary passengers, and that dangers apply also to them, particularly instanced by the working of the quarry on the cliff'. Despite Mr. Head's concern, the railway opened to goods traffic on 1 October 1900.

The anxiety about the quarrying on the cliffs above the railway (it seems that there was particular concern over Shepherd's Dinner Quarry, near Church Ope Cove) proved to be justified. There were regular rockfalls - most were very minor, but in September 1901 a block weighing an estimated 10 tons fell on to the permanent way. Although nobody was hurt, and the line was still not open for passenger traffic, the Portland Local Board notified the E&CHR of its grave concern: '....such quarry workings cannot be allowed by the side of a passenger railway - if necessary by an injunction. The quarry men have also _blasted_ there!!'

Later, a solution to the problem came in the form of 'rock signals'. At each end of the 'danger' section, a home signal was kept permanently in the 'off' position by wires, stretched between the cliffs and the track, something after the manner of a high fence. If a rock were to fall, it would break the wires causing the signals to return to 'danger'. (A better known example of 'rock signals' was on the Oban line).

Ubiquity..... O2 No.177 (later BR No.30177), the first of the class to be built, waits at Easton with the 5.17pm to Weymouth on 28 May 1929. The engine seems to have lost the glass from its cab window. PHOTOGRAPH: H.C. CASSERLEY

A fine portrait of O2 No.221 at Easton. This locomotive was a long-term resident at Dorchester, and was regularly used on the Easton branch. The photograph can be dated between February 1932, when the loco lost its 'E' prefix ('E' for Eastleigh, the 'home workshops' of ex-LSWR locos) and July 1948, when it had its BR number (30221) applied.

Towards Completion

In 1901 work at last commenced to bring the Admiralty Line up to standard so that passenger services could be introduced. It was inspected by Colonel Yorke in March 1902, who noted that it was: '....*34.6 chains, single throughout; the steepest gradient is 1 in 48.24 and the sharpest curve 10½ chains .... permanent way is similar to that of the Easton & Church Hope Railway .... the one underbridge has been reconstructed with steel plate girders and trough flooring....*' The works, which had cost the E&CHR £4,419, were considered satisfactory, but permission to open to passenger traffic was refused. This was partly because of the faulty operation of the ground frame at the Portland end of the line - the electric train staff could be removed while the points were open - but principally because there was still no station at the northern end of the line (under the existing layout, E&CHR trains could not gain direct access to Portland station).

There was a further reinspection of the Admiralty Line on 14 August 1902, and this time the verdict was favourable. The inspection took in a temporary station at Portland, which had been erected on a siding at the northern end of the Admiralty Line adjacent to the site of the future through station. This temporary station was on a very sharp (5 chain) curve, but this was not objected to as: '....*this is the end of the line and the speed of trains must of necessity be low*'. There was a new signal box containing 17 levers - 15 in use and 2 spare - for working the points of the run-round loop.

The facilities at the temporary station comprised: '*A single platform and waiting shed .... but has neither booking office nor convenience of any kind*'. In his report Colonel Yorke recorded that: '....*passengers for Weymouth will have to change, and walk by a footpath, fenced and raised but not covered, to the old terminus of the Weymouth & Portland Railway. This arrangement cannot be regarded as satisfactory, being highly inconvenient, and not likely to encourage passengers to make use of the new railway (the E&CHR) to the summit of the island....*' The report expressed hope that: '....*this will encourage the swift completion of a new station to accommodate all three companies to take the place of the miserable structure belonging to the Weymouth & Portland Railway.*'

Colonel Yorke was quick to criticise: '....*instead of erecting a new station, the Railway companies have spent money on the temporary platform, which would have been more usefully expended on the much needed permanent station .... the complainants* [regarding the old Portland station] *have been told that, as soon as the difficulty regarding the site* [for a new station] *was removed, a new station was to be built. Now, however, that site is available, no use has been made of it and the companies have done nothing beyond building an open platform with a small shed on it (for the use only of passengers to and from Easton) on land which has all along belonged to them*'. Overall, the report smacked of exasperation.

The E&CHR finally opened to passenger traffic on 1 September 1902. Given that the company had been formed in 1867, this must surely have been one of the longest gestation periods of any British railway company. From the travelling public's point of view, matters improved considerably in 1905 when, at very long last, a new through station was opened at Portland. This - and other twentieth century matters - will be discussed in the next chapter...

At Easton, the end of the line was very final indeed - it ended in this cutting ¼-mile north of the passenger station. PHOTOGRAPH: H.C. CASSERLEY

Above. In 1905 the travelling public of Portland finally got a new station. It was open and airy - or to put it another way, downright draughty. In this undated view, O2 No.207 stands at the down platform, presumably with a train which has terminated here; the locomotive appears to have run round its train and is ready to return bunker-first to Weymouth. Note the wooden construction of the platforms. PHOTOGRAPH: J. SMITH

Below. The obligatory line-up of staff at Portland station, but there must be some absentees as, until the 1930s, over twenty persons were employed there. This view looks towards the site of the old terminus, the yard of which can just be discerned in the distance. PHOTOGRAPH: J. SMITH

Chapter Five
The Twentieth Century

As we have already seen, the original railway station at Portland was hugely unpopular with the travelling public. Despite repeated prodding from the local authorities and the Board of Trade throughout the 1890s, the Weymouth & Portland Railway managed to evade the issue until the early 1900s. The company was finally goaded into action by the opening, in 1902, of the Easton & Church Hope Railway to passenger traffic. As related earlier, the E&CHR was provided with a temporary through platform at Portland, but the W&PR, seemingly defiant to the last, did not actually complete the permanent station for virtually three more years.

At long last, the new through station was ready for the obligatory Board of Trade inspection, on 28 June 1905. The inspecting officer was Colonel Yorke who, by this time, must have been rather familiar with the area. The report explained that: *'The railway is single, but the station forms a passing place, with up and down lines and two platforms each 400ft long which are connected by a footbridge. On the down side a general waiting room and conveniences for men are provided, and on the up side there is complete waiting and lavatory accommodation for both sexes. The station is on a curve of 7½ chains radius .... both lines are fitted with check rails, and as all trains stop at this station, the curve must not be objected to. There are two new signal boxes, viz:- Portland Station box containing 16 levers in use and 5 spare levers and Portland Goods Junction box containing 21 levers in use and 6 spare levers.'*

It appears that the new station at Portland had actually become operational on Sunday 7 May 1905 - seven weeks before the official inspection. The opening of a station or new works in advance of a BoT inspection was not particularly unusual. In such cases, an inspecting officer had usually given a verbal 'all clear' at the earlier date, subject to any necessary works being carried out. However, given the W&PR's record, one might have expected Colonel Yorke to have exercised extreme caution, and not to have placed any reliance on the railway company. With the opening of the new station at Portland in May 1905, the much detested old station was officially closed to passengers and relegated to the status of a goods shed. In fact, it was widely opined that, for many years, the station had been no better than a goods shed.....

With the opening of the new station at Portland the entire Weymouth - Easton line, although owned by two separate companies, was worked as one. The new station was wholly owned by the W&PR, and so the E&CHR had to pay a rent of £6 per month for the privilege of using it.

Although it was good news for Portland's travelling public in the early 1900s, it was not such good news for the E&CHR. In 1908, as a result of an action brought by Debenture holders, the company was placed in the hands of a Receiver. Nevertheless, it managed to continue operating in Receivership until the end of 1947.

General Improvements
Ever since the Weymouth & Portland line had opened in 1865, the timber viaducts across the Backwater at Weymouth and across the East Fleet had been viewed, by the travelling public, with a degree of caution. In some cases, with extreme caution. As the years progressed, the structures attracted increasingly vociferous criticism, but it was the 1900s before either was replaced. The first to be dealt with was the East Fleet Viaduct, replaced in 1902 by a nine-span plate girder structure on a parallel alignment. The new viaduct had a shorter overall span than its predecessor - 120 yards instead of 198 yards.

In 1909 the Backwater Viaduct was replaced. As related earlier, it had had to be substantially rebuilt even before the railway had opened, but in the thirty-four years since, had received little more than routine maintenance. Whereas the original viaduct was 489 yards in length, the replacement was only 180 yards. This huge reduction in length was made possible by building approach embankments at each end of the viaduct - at the Weymouth end there was a 230 yard embankment, and at the Portland end one of 80 yards. (The embankment at the Portland end was pierced by a brick arch of 25ft span.) The embankments were formed of Portland stone rubble, some 30,000 tons of it - most of this rubble had come from Easton.

The viaduct itself comprised five spans of lattice work steel girders, each of 108ft span; these were supported by cast iron cylinders 8ft in diameter below ground, tapering to 6ft above ground, sunk into the river bed at depths of between 17ft and 32ft below low water. For added stability, the cylinders were filled with concrete. The whole structure was on a 30-chain curve, and was on a uniform gradient of 1 in 113, rising towards Portland. It was actually built alongside the old viaduct - this, clearly, was to enable a normal train service to operate while the work was in progress. The new viaduct was brought into use on 1 February 1909; as had been the case with the East Fleet Viaduct, the cost of construction had been borne by the GWR.

At the northern end of Backwater Viaduct was a new station. This was Melcombe Regis, which had a single platform 400ft in length. It stood on land reclaimed from the Backwater, the infilling having been done with chalk, some 20,000 tons of which had been specially excavated near Dorchester. This new station opened on 30 May 1909. Its importance was that most Portland branch trains subsequently started and terminated there instead of at the main line station. This was a much needed solution to the age-old problem of delays - not to mention dangers - of shunting branch trains across the main line to and from Weymouth station. However, from the railway companies' point of view there was another side to the coin; although Melcombe Regis station was only 200 yards from the main line station at Weymouth, that distance was enough to discourage a number of passengers - particularly the elderly and infirm - from making through journeys.

In Southern Railway days, after the station platforms had been rebuilt in concrete, an unidentified O2 waits with its train at the down platform at Portland. Presumably, this train operated only to/from Portland - if it had originated at Easton, one might expect to see it at the other platform. It has been suggested that this was an Easton-bound motor train - i.e. it was being driven from the leading coach - but as far as can be determined the Dorchester O2s used on the Easton branch were not actually motor fitted. **PHOTOGRAPH: J. SMITH**

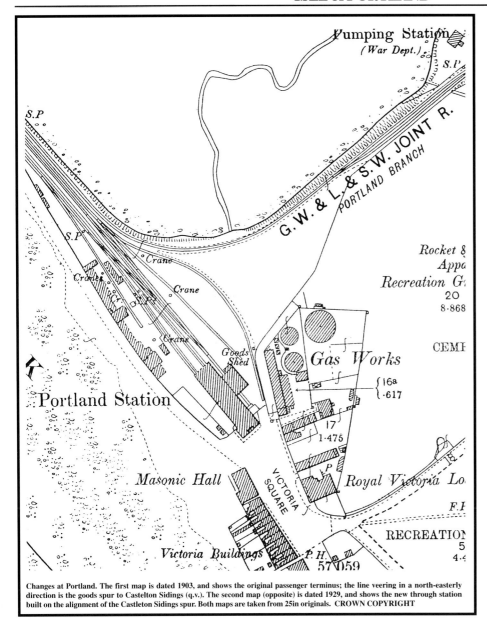

Changes at Portland. The first map is dated 1903, and shows the original passenger terminus; the line veering in a north-easterly direction is the goods spur to Castelton Sidings (q.v.). The second map (opposite) is dated 1929, and shows the new through station built on the alignment of the Castleton Sidings spur. Both maps are taken from 25in originals. **CROWN COPYRIGHT**

A 'Burrell Road Locomotive', owned by the Bath & Portland Stone Firms Ltd, hauling two trailers of stone somewhere near Easton in April 1930. A splendid photograph...... **PHOTOGRAPH: BRITISH GEOLOGICAL SURVEY**

Other improvements of the period included the provision of a passing loop and the erection of a second platform at Rodwell in December 1907, and the opening of Westham halt and Wyke Regis halt (the latter principally for the benefit of workers at Whiteheads Torpedo Factory), both on 1 July 1909. The platforms at Westham and Wyke Regis were lengthened in February 1913.

During the Great War the Weymouth - Portland section, in particular, was intensively used, due principally to the importance of the Admiralty establishment at Portland Harbour. Wyke Regis halt also saw a significant increase in traffic, primarily in connection with the nearby torpedo factory.

The Grouping

The Railways Act of 1921 resulted in the formation of the 'big four' railway companies. This, of course, was what is usually referred to as the Grouping. The two local companies on the Isle of Portland - the Weymouth & Portland Railway and the Easton & Church Hope Railway - retained their corporate independence, although the 'new' joint operators of the lines logically became the GWR and the Southern Railway (the Southern having absorbed the LSWR).

The E&CHR, although remaining independent, was still in receivership - indeed it was to continue in this manner until Nationalisation in 1948 - and this meant that its every financial move was closely scrutinised. In an attempt to keep a necessarily tight rein on matters, it had to vigorously pursue every last penny to which it considered itself entitled. This it did - often to the irritation of the other companies with whom it was involved.

One of the E&CHR's perennial disputes was with the operating companies, especially regarding its proportion of receipts and the manner in which they were paid. For example, in February 1924 the Southern Railway wrote to the E&CHR announcing that it was about to send the account for the E&CHR's proportion of traffic receipts for the first half year of 1923. However, the SR explained that a deduction had to be made for the cost of installing a set of catch points at Easton, and advised the E&CHR that interest on the capital cost would be charged. The E&CHR promptly replied to the SR: '....you can hardly claim to charge interest on the capital expenditure unless you are prepared to pay interest on net receipts, which you have, without any justification, retained in hand six months beyond the date provided for in the Agreement.'

That matter might be considered relatively trivial - after all, the amount of interest involved was not vast - but it was symptomatic of the perpetual niggles between the E&CHR and the working companies. It became quite predictable that, whenever each half-year's accounts were received, the E&CHR would find a cause for querying this, that or the other. The Southern Railway's patience clearly wore a little thin for, after receiving yet another query in March 1932, it enquired of the E&CHR why it is: '....necessary for you to object each half-year to the basis upon which a settlement is made'. By this time, the Receiver in charge of the E&CHR's affairs was Mr. L.J. Evans, the original Receiver, Arthur Lemon, having died in 1928.

Part of the E&CHR's problem was that it was tied to the original working agreement of 1897, whereby it was worked by the GWR and LSWR for a fixed amount of 2/6d per train-mile, rather than a percentage proportion of receipts as was often the case elsewhere. By the 1930s, the perils of a 'fixed rate' agreement were clearly seen - motor bus services had cut swathes into local railway traffic, and the railway companies (not only on Portland, but all over Britain) had often found it necessary to run more trains, often with reduced fares, in order to compete. But the E&CHR still had to pay the SR the same amount, regardless of whether the trains ran near-full or near-empty, and irrespective of the fares charged. To illustrate the scale of the E&CHR's problem - at Easton, in 1929 a total of 1,080 passenger tickets was issued for receipts of £304, while in 1933 the sale of 1,274 tickets realised only £223.

During the mid-1930s the E&CHR's expenses exceeded receipts by between £1,200 and £1,500 per annum. In an attempt to rectify this situation, the company asked the SR to review the number of services '....to see whether there is a proper and reasonable justification for running all the trains'. The SR replied that, as the joint working company, it was under a legal obligation '....to work the railway so as to develop the traffic, and to run proper and sufficient trains'. However, the SR subsequently agreed to an experimental revision of services - for the winter of 1937/38 the number of weekday passenger workings each way between Portland and Easton were reduced from seven to five. The experiment proved worthwhile, and the 'axed' trains were never reinstated.

Although the withdrawal of two passenger trains each day saved the E&CHR the best part of £400 p.a. in working expenses, this was nowhere near enough to bring the balance sheet into the black. By the end of 1938, its debt to the Admiralty alone was a whopping £14,480 - made up principally of unpaid bills for the use of the Admiralty line between Portland and Castletown.

During World War II the E&CHR and W&PR - along with *all* the railway companies in Britain - came under Government control. The Weymouth - Portland section saw fairly heavy use, especially in connection with the

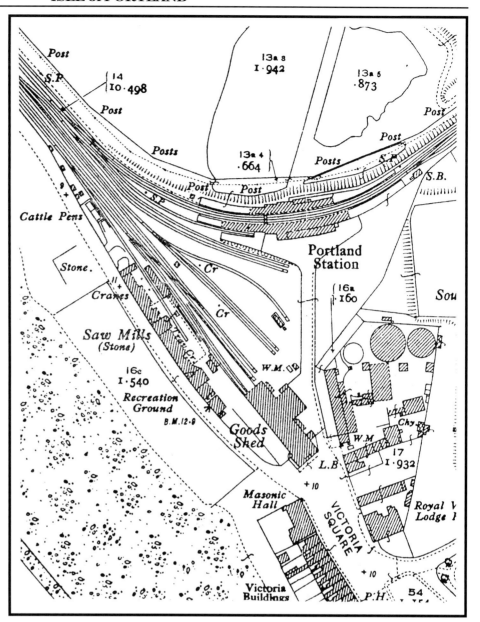

Quarrying had a huge effect on everyday life on Portland and, inevitably, was allied to railway development - and fortunes - on the island. This is Suckthumb Quarry, to the south-west of Easton, in April 1930. It was not actually connected to the E&CHR, the tracks seen here were simply to transport heavy blocks of stone from the face to a point of transhipment. PHOTOGRAPH: BRITISH GEOLOGICAL SURVEY

Naval base at Portland, but the traffic on the Portland - Easton section was not greatly affected.

State Ownership

On 1 January 1948 the Easton & Church Hope and the Weymouth & Portland Railways finally lost their independence when, along with the GWR and SR, they became part of British Railways. By this time, the general lack of passenger traffic affected not only the Easton section but the entire branch. Almost inevitably, the lack of patronage did not go unnoticed by BR, and all passenger services were withdrawn as from Monday 3 March 1952. The 'last rites' were conducted the previous Saturday with O2 0-4-4Ts Nos.30177 and 30197 hauling six WR corridor coaches, well filled with enthusiasts. The last day of public services - Sunday 2 March - was rather more sedate with O2 No.30177 hauling the SR articulated set which had been transferred to the branch from the Isle of Sheppey line, following the latter's closure to passengers in December 1950. It did not go unremarked that the ex-Sheppey set therefore saw two closures in just sixteen months.

There was no question of the branch closing completely - the stone traffic from Easton had diminished, but the traffic to and from the Naval base at Portland, in particular, was still fairly steady. The Melcombe Regis end of the branch proved very useful for empty stock storage; this had been a long-standing problem in the Weymouth area especially, of course, on summer Saturdays and at other holiday times. Even the remodelling of Weymouth station in 1956/57 was unable to solve the problem of peak season stock storage.

During the mid- and late 1950s it was occasionally necessary to use Melcombe Regis station as a peak season 'overflow' for the adja-

Top right. **Melcombe Regis station, which opened in 1909 - note the original timber platform. Judging by the freshness of the ballast, it is quite possible that this picture was taken very soon after the station opened. The locomotive appears to be a GWR 0-6-0ST, which would seem to confirm a very early date. Weymouth goods yard can be seen in the distance. PHOTOGRAPH: J. SMITH**

Middle right. **At Portland, a new signal box was provided just to the north of the station in October 1935, but was destroyed by enemy bombing, in the preliminary offensive to the Battle of Britain proper, on 11 August 1940. A replacement box opened on an adjacent site on 28 September 1941. The new box - seen here on 27 March 1965 - had 33 levers; after the withdrawal of passenger services in 1952 it opened only from 8.00am to 4.00pm. Between here and Easton, working was by electric train staff until April 1955, when it was replaced by wooden train staff (for 'one engine in steam' working). The Portland - Rodwell section was worked by electric key token. The box remained operational until the complete closure of the branch on 5 April 1965 - latterly, it had been open from 9.50am to 4.50pm. PHOTOGRAPH: COLIN CADDY**

Bottom right. **Having passed under the Buxton Road bridge, O2 No.30197 starts the descent to Rodwell station. The date is 11 July 1951. PHOTOGRAPH: R.H. TUNSTALL**

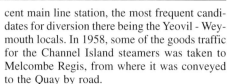

cent main line station, the most frequent candidates for diversion there being the Yeovil - Weymouth locals. In 1958, some of the goods traffic for the Channel Island steamers was taken to Melcombe Regis, from where it was conveyed to the Quay by road.

In the early 1960s, it was not unknown for Melcombe Regis to be used by Channel Island boat trains. One such occasion was on 15 July 1961 when the M.V.SARNIA, having been seriously delayed by gales, arrived from the Channel Islands some eight hours late. Under normal circumstances the boat train would have left Weymouth Quay at 5.55am, but when the boat finally arrived a little after midday, it was impossible for a train to meet it as three down boat trains were scheduled at the Quay, thus occupying all three platforms. The alternative was to transport the SARNIA's passengers by 'bus to Melcombe Regis, from where the boat train finally departed at 1.10pm.

At this time, there were still daily freight workings to and from Portland and Easton, but from June 1964 the freight services between Portland and Easton ran only when required. Less than a year later - on 5 April 1965 - the scheduled freight services to Portland were withdrawn, although special trains were run the following week to clear remaining wagons from the branch. When these had been cleared, the section of the branch southwards from the Westham end of the Backwater Viaduct was taken out of use. At this time, the branch was just six months away from its centenary.

The Melcombe Regis end of the line - including Backwater Viaduct itself - remained in use for wagon storage until 10 January 1966. Six weeks later, on 26 February 1966, stop blocks were placed across the branch in Weymouth station yard. This was the very end for the last surviving section of the Portland branch.

Top left. **In 1962, WR 0-6-0PT No.4689 prepares to take on water at Easton. The pile of rubble in the foreground was once an engine shed..... Ten years have elapsed since the cessation of passenger services, but the station building itself seems substantially intact. A tribute to the quality of the local stone, no doubt. PHOTOGRAPH: COLIN CADDY**

Middle left. **Traffic on the Portland branch might have decreased by 1962, but that certainly didn't mean that permanent way work could be ignored. This lengthy p.w. train on Chesil Beach causeway was photographed on 2 September 1962. The locomotive is No.7780. PHOTOGRAPH: COLIN CADDY**

Bottom left. **Ivatt 2-6-2T No.41293 passes through the remains of Portland passenger station on its way back from Easton to Weymouth on 6 February 1965. PHOTOGRAPH: COLIN CADDY**

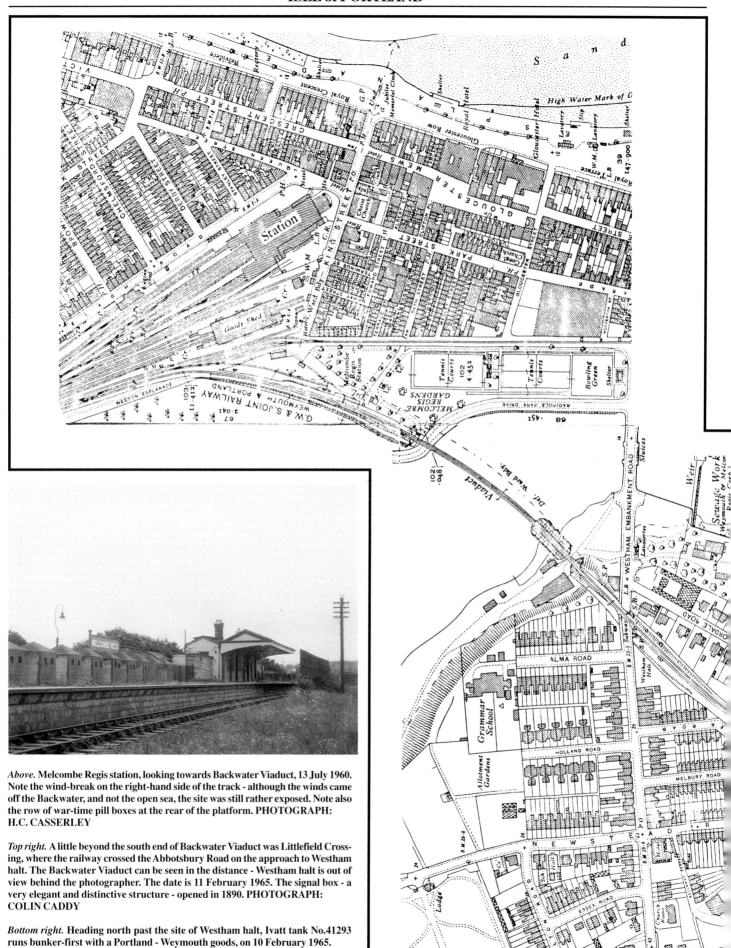

Above. Melcombe Regis station, looking towards Backwater Viaduct, 13 July 1960. Note the wind-break on the right-hand side of the track - although the winds came off the Backwater, and not the open sea, the site was still rather exposed. Note also the row of war-time pill boxes at the rear of the platform. PHOTOGRAPH: H.C. CASSERLEY

Top right. A little beyond the south end of Backwater Viaduct was Littlefield Crossing, where the railway crossed the Abbotsbury Road on the approach to Westham halt. The Backwater Viaduct can be seen in the distance - Westham halt is out of view behind the photographer. The date is 11 February 1965. The signal box - a very elegant and distinctive structure - opened in 1890. PHOTOGRAPH: COLIN CADDY

Bottom right. Heading north past the site of Westham halt, Ivatt tank No.41293 runs bunker-first with a Portland - Weymouth goods, on 10 February 1965. PHOTOGRAPH: COLIN CADDY

Chapter Six

The Route

N.B: The Ordnance Survey maps featured here are reduced from their original scale of 25in to 1 mile. Please note that not all of the maps are from the same survey. The dates for each section are as follows:
Weymouth-Marsh Road - 1929
Marsh Road-Sandsfoot Castle - 1912
Sandsfoot Castle-Ferrybridge - 1929
Chesil Beach-Balaclava Bay - 1929
Balaclava Bay-Wakeham Quarries - 1903
Wakeham Quarries-Easton section - 1929

Starting from the northern end, the Portland branch diverged from the main line some 600 yards to the north of Weymouth station, at a point referred to as Portland Junction. The junction was originally at the western extremity of the station yard, but in the mid-1930s two sets of sidings - the Jubillee (sic) and Jersey sidings - were added on the west side of the junction, thereby sandwiching the head of the branch line between the Quay Tramway and the new sidings.

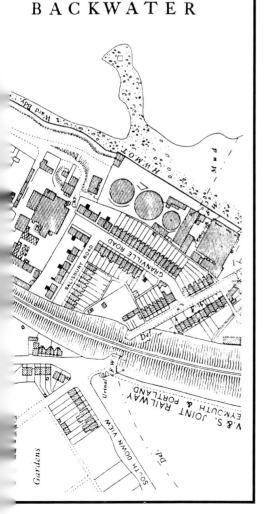

BACKWATER

As already explained - repeatedly! - the original edict was that branch trains had to be hauled between the junction and the station. In other words, the engines of branch trains had to run round at the junction. This unpopular practice virtually ceased in 1909 with the opening, on 30 May of that year, of **Melcombe Regis station** (27 chains from the junction) on the branch 200 yards from the main line station. That said, the purpose-built embankment on which the station stood was actually on a slightly different alignment to that of the original branch line; during the general improvements in 1909, the new embankment to carry the railway was constructed *alongside* (i.e. not on the same alignment) as the original track-bed. Another aspect of the 1909 improvements was the construction of a subway under the line at the southern end of the station - the subway carried a pedestrian footpath and, as its floor level was below that of high water, it was provided with a non-flooding tidal valve. The station approach road was, in effect, a continuation of King Street, in which the main line station was situated.

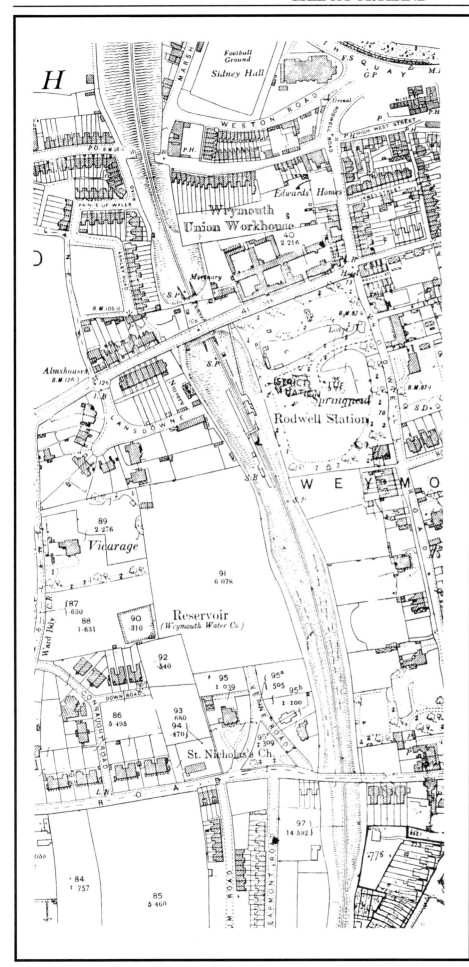

Melcombe Regis station had a single platform 400ft in length; originally, the facing edge of the platform was built of timber, but in Southern Railway days was reconstructed in stone and concrete. A distinctive feature of the station platform was the row of pill boxes, a reminder of the area's strategic importance - and potential targeting - during the War.

At the southern end of Melcombe Regis station was Backwater Viaduct. As related earlier, the original timber viaduct of 1864 was replaced on 1 February 1909 by a steel structure on a parallel alignment. New approach embankments were built at each end of the new viaduct, thereby reducing the overall span from 489 to 180 yards.

After leaving the viaduct, the railway continued on a ruling gradient of 1 in 96 (rising), crossing the Abbotsbury Road on the level and then entering **Westham halt** (49 chains from the junction at Weymouth). The halt opened on 1 July 1909, and its single platform was extended in February 1913. At its northern end, the railway crossed Abbotsbury Road on the level - this was referred to as Littlefield Crossing. Following the lengthening of the platform at Westham halt in 1913, Dorset County Council alleged that the W&PR had encroached into the road and insisted that the railway company set back its fences and gates and restore the road surface - an exercise estimated at £500. The W&PR replied that nothing had been altered during the recent works, and if there were any sort of encroachment, it had existed ever since the railway had opened. The railway dismissed the Council's claim as being: '....barred by lapse of time and acquiescence'. The Council subsequently adopted a tougher stance, at which point the W&PR passed the buck to the GWR and LSWR, to whom the line was leased.

The matter dragged on until 1917, when it was finally agreed that, for the benefit of pedestrians (in lieu of restricted access caused by the alleged encroachment), a subway should be constructed under the railway adjacent to the crossing. This was eventually done - the subway cost an estimated £1,500, of which the County Council paid £500 and the railway companies the rest. It had taken over four years.....

Southwards from Westham halt, the line continued climbing, now on a ruling gradient of 1 in 58 and carried by the massive Marsh Embankment over Newstead Road. Because of the scale of the embankment, the road underbridge was more like a short tunnel. Continuing on the embankment, the railway crossed Chickerell Road and then burrowed under Wyke Road by means of a 58 yard tunnel. It had been built to accommodate a double line of broad gauge track.

Just beyond the south end of the tunnel, in a cutting, was **Rodwell station** (1m 16ch), which opened in May 1870 to become the first intermediate station on the line. Rodwell originally had only one platform - this was on the east side (despite what seems to be shown on contemporary Ordnance Survey maps!) and was equipped with a sturdy stone-built waiting room. A small timber signal box was provided in December 1892. A passing loop and second platform were added (and the original platform lengthened) in December 1907, and the origi-

The massive Marsh Embankment carried the line above the Westham area of Weymouth and over Newstead Road, the road bridge actually being more akin to a short tunnel. On 21 January 1965, Ivatt tank No.41324 runs bunker-first with the Portland - Weymouth goods. **PHOTOGRAPH: COLIN CADDY**

nal signal box was replaced by a new brick-built box on the second (up) platform. ,

Continuing southwards from Rodwell the line remained in a cutting, passing through what was, in the 1800s, fairly open countryside. The railway then passed under what was originally known as Buxton Lane (later Buxton Road), near which was the summit of the Weymouth - Portland section. From this point, one could see westwards along the coast to the Golden Cap near Bridport, eastwards to St. Aldhem's Head on the Isle of Purbeck, northwards towards the hills around Dorchester, and southwards across the Chesil Beach towards the Isle of Portland.

Just to the south of Buxton Lane bridge the railway emerged from the cutting and embarked on a descent - on a ruling gradient of 1 in 66 -

towards **Sandsfoot Castle halt** (1m 53ch), a simple platform which opened on 1 August 1932. The line continued, partly on embankment and partly in cutting, only a few yards from the shore to **Wyke Regis halt** (2m 29ch). This halt opened on 1 July 1909, at which time Wyke Regis was an almost completely rural area - somewhat different from today! The original purpose of the halt was to serve the nearby torpedo works of Messrs. Whitehead & Co., and when the works had been constructed in the late 1880s/early 1890s, the transportation of building materials had sometimes caused delays to the passenger trains. Given the wholesale public dissatisfaction with the operation of the branch at that time, the delays caused by the construction work had only made things worse.

Wyke Regis halt had a single wooden platform and an archetypal GWR-pattern pagoda-style shelter. A longer platform was provided in February 1913, presumably in anticipation of increased traffic to/from the torpedo works. A siding to the works was installed in the early 1890s, and additional siding accommodation was provided during the Great War, when production was stepped up. The torpedo works had an internal 2ft gauge tramway (this appears to have been installed during World War I) which, from 1929, was worked by a four-wheeled battery electric locomotive. The works tramway extended to a lengthy pier, along which torpedoes were taken for testing in the harbour. The factory became part of the Vickers Armstrong empire in June 1944, and remained operational until 1967.

South of Wyke Regis, the Portland branch crossed the Fleet Water on a viaduct. As related earlier, the original timber viaduct was replaced in 1902 by a plate girder structure - the new viaduct was on a slightly different alignment, and the approaches at either end were built up so that the overall span was reduced. During World War II the deck of the viaduct was laid as a roadway for emergency use. The decking was taken out of use in December 1946.

From the southern end of the viaduct the railway negotiated the causeway formed by Chesil Beach. On the causeway the line was almost at sea level, and at this point was extremely exposed to the vagaries of Portland Bay on one side and West Bay on the other. Indeed, during gales in October 1949 the sea swept over the causeway and undermined the track to such an extent that a GWR 57XX 0-6-0PT (presumably on a goods working) plunged through the tracks. The line had to be closed for a time while rock in-filling was substituted.

Having crossed the causeway the railway entered **Portland station** (4m 29ch), the original terminus of the line. As we have seen, when the E&CHR opened to passenger traffic in September 1902 a temporary platform was provided on the new through line while, much to the relief of the local travelling public, a new through station (4m 25ch from Weymouth Junction) was brought into use in May 1905. The through station was on a passing loop and had two platforms - the original platforms were constructed of timber, but in Southern Railway days these were replaced by platforms built of stone and concrete. The new station was purposely constructed two feet above the level of the old one in order to prevent the possibility of flooding, which had been an occasional problem at the old station. The raising of the level, although by just a couple of feet, required an additional 4,000 tons of rubble.

With the opening of the new through station in 1905, the old, much-derided terminus at the rear of the through station remained in use as a goods depot.

From the 'new' station, the branch line headed in an easterly direction, preparing to hug the coast on its way to Easton. About 15 chains beyond Portland station - at a point referred to as Castletown Junction - the railway started to traverse what was once the Admiralty line. At the junction, a siding diverged and provided an

Rodwell station in double-platform days, with what appears to be a GWR 2021 class 0-6-0ST heading a Portland - bound passenger train. **PHOTOGRAPH: LENS OF SUTTON**

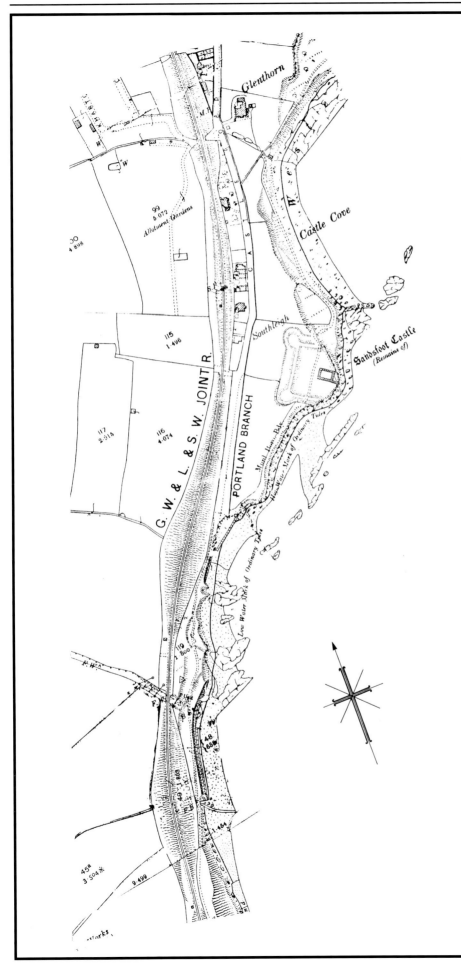

interchange with the old 4ft 6in gauge Portland Railway (the 'Merchants Tramway'). At the interchange point - known as Castleton Sidings - there were two gantry cranes for the unloading of stone from the tramway wagons to the railway company wagons. One of these gantries - a 12-ton affair - was provided about 1904 '....at an estimated cost of £291 less about £15 for the materials to be obtained from an old 5-ton gantry which will be removed'. As will be seen from the accompanying maps, sidings from the Merchants Tramway also diverged to the pier at Castletown - these, of course, predated the exchange sidings.

Close to the bridge which carried the Easton line over the foot of the tramway incline was **Hospital halt** (4m 48ch), a private halt which served the nearby Naval hospital. Contemporary maps show only a single platform at this halt, but photographs clearly show two platforms. The branch line then hugged the lower part of the slope above the massive Naval Dockyard at Portland. The dockyard had its own internal railway system which was connected to the Easton branch at Admiralty Extension Junction - this was, in fact, the point at which the E&CHR joined the old Admiralty Line. While passing the eastern end of the dockyard, the Easton line was conveyed by a viaduct across a rope-worked incline to Grove Quarries.

From here on, the line began its climb towards Portland on a ruling gradient of a ferocious 1 in 40. Around much of the east coast of Portland, the railway ran on a rocky shelf between the massive cliffs and the sea. There was once a proposal to build a station on this section, principally for serving the prison, but it was not acted upon.

Shortly before reaching Church Ope Cove the line turned inland through a sheer-sided rock cutting, passing under Wakeham Street (at the southern end of Easton) by means of a bridge almost adjacent to the *Mermaid Inn*. A little way beyond the bridge the Quarry Tip siding joined by means of a trailing connection from the left - this siding was on the alignment of the original (uncompleted) E&CHR of the late 1860s. Quarry Tip siding crossed Pennsylvania Road on the level, and continued to the top of the cliffs alongside Southwell Road. It remained in situ until around 1956 having, over the years, gained private sidings diverging to the Bath & Portland Stone Co. (first siding 1904, later siding 1940) and the Easton & South Western Stone Co. (siding agreement dated 7 September 1933).

In 1902 the E&CHR contemplated extending the Quarry Tip siding for a distance of about 10 chains to Messrs. Webber & Pangbourne's quarry at Dunscroft. The estimated cost of the extension was £100, but as the quarry company had already signed an agreement to dispatch all its stone by the E&CHR - with or without the extension - the railway company viewed the outlay as unnecessary and so the extension did not materialise.

From the point where Quarry Tip siding joined the branch line, the railway curved north towards Easton - this final ascent to the station was on a ferocious 1 in 44 gradient. On this section were private sidings to Bottom Combe Quarry (into use 17 April 1924) and Park Quarry

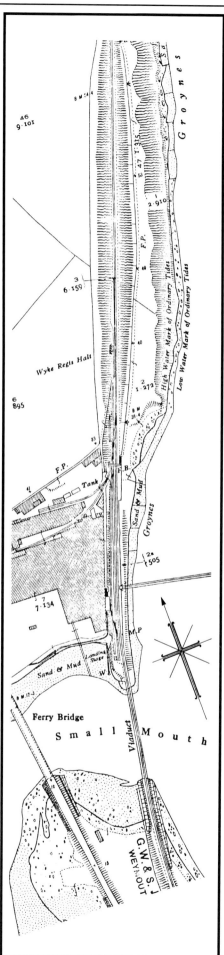

Top. **Wyke Regis halt, with its simple platform and minimal facilities, opened in 1909. The locomotive at the head of the Portland-bound train looks suspiciously like a LSWR C14 motor train engine which, given the LSWR's unsuccessful foray with steam railmotors on the line in 1909, might possibly have been tried as an alternative. However, the train in this picture appears to consist of at least four coaches, and it is unlikely that a diminutive C14 would have been required to bring that sort of load up from Weymouth. PHOTOGRAPH: J. SMITH**

Above. **Hugging the coast on the approach to Sandsfoot Castle halt, O2 No.30223 heads a Weymouth - Portland train on 13 July 1951. PHOTOGRAPH: R.H. TUNSTALL**

(Messrs. Webber & Pangbourne - siding agreement 30 October 1903). The latter actually diverged from the yard of **Easton station** (7m 47ch from Weymouth Junction), which has frequently been described as 'a modeller's dream'. The original station building was largely destroyed by fire on 28 November 1903 - only a little over a year after it had opened - and was not rebuilt until 1904. It boasted a single platform with run-round loop, a small goods yard and a single-road engine shed. The shed was jointly owned by the GWR and LSWR; it opened in February 1905 - i.e. five years after goods traffic commenced on the Easton section - and although officially closed in 1925, remained in use as a stabling point until at least 1950 or 1951.

The goods yard at Easton station was originally equipped with a 2½-ton portable crane, but in 1928 a new 6-ton fixed hand crane was installed. The new piece, which cost £335, had ac-

tually been ordered by the GWR for the goods yard at Wellington, but was diverted to Easton.

The station was a few yards to the west of Easton Square, and was reached by an access road from Reforne Street. Beyond the north end of the station the branch continued for a little over ¼-mile (as a mineral line) under Reforne Street, terminating in a solid rock cutting 7 miles 75 chains from Weymouth Junction. This final section had sidings to a coal wharf and a quarry. The coal wharf was brought into use in 1904 - a couple of years earlier, the local coal merchants had threatened to boycott the railway if they were placed under an obligation to use the wharf, but the conflict had been avoided. The sidings to the quarry were the subject of an agreement dated 14 August 1902. Safety catch points were provided on the running line to protect trains in the station from quarry wagons which might break loose. There was also a Board of Trade edict that: '....owing to the gradient all traffic to

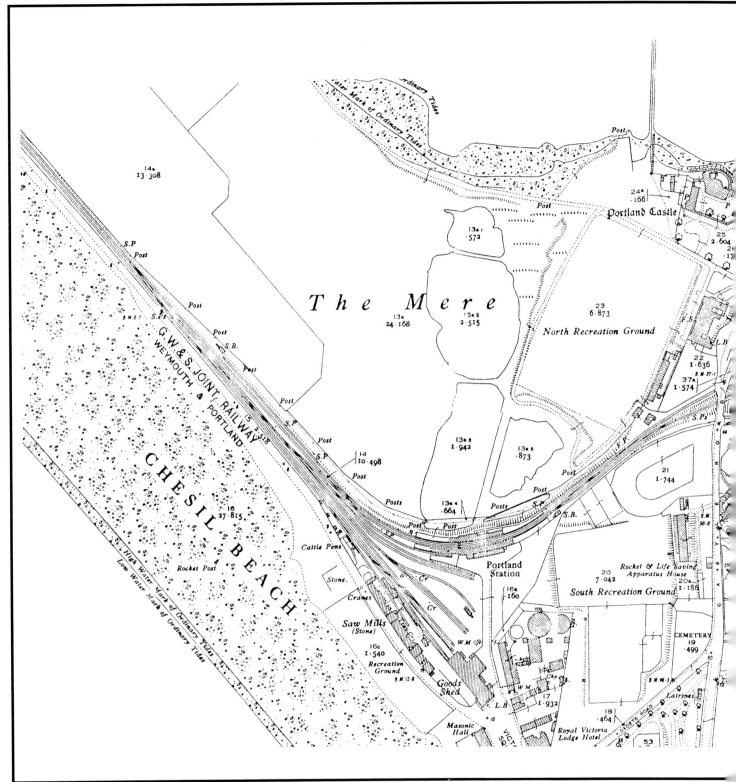

and from the siding must be worked by an engine from Easton station, and no wagons must be allowed to stand on the main line without an engine at their lower end'. Interestingly, that BoT stipulation referred to the quarry siding as 'Palmers Siding', although other sources refer to 'Sheepcroft Sidings'. Whatever their correct identity, they appear to have been removed prior to 1950.

Today

By way of a brief footnote, it should be mentioned that some parts of the route of the Weymouth - Portland - Easton branch are still clearly discernible today. That said, the section through the town of Weymouth has largely disappeared - an almost inevitable consequence of urban development - but to the south of the town it is a happier story for railway archaeologists and keen walkers. The Fleet Viaduct might have been dismantled, but its approaches are easily made out, while beyond the viaduct, the track-bed parallel with the road along Chesil Beach is now a public footpath. The site of Portland station has been more or less obliterated by redevelopment and the route of the railway through the Navy premises has largely disappeared. A welcome survival for the railway historian, however, is the alignment of the old 4ft 6in gauge Portland Tramway and its inclines above Fortuneswell, which remain undeveloped. The section of the old tramway beneath Verne Citadel is now a designated public footpath, and the course of the incline down to Castletown is still clearly discernible, although somewhat overgrown. Around the east coast of the island the

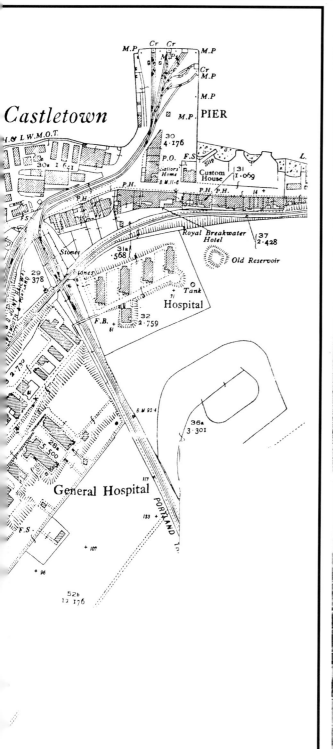

Top. East Fleet Viaduct, viewed from the northern end on 8 February 1965. The bridge was also known locally as Ferrybridge, the nearby road bridge (just visible through the piers of the railway bridge) having opened in 1839 to replace a ferry across the East Fleet. PHOTOGRAPH: COLIN CADDY

Middle. The famous Chesil Beach, viewed from the east on 13 February 1965. The road across the Chesil was on the other side of the railway embankment. A Portland-bound goods is headed by Ivatt 2-6-2T No.41293. PHOTOGRAPH: COLIN CADDY

Bottom. Looking across from the Chesil towards Portland - the goods depot (the old passenger terminus) is right of centre, while the through passenger station of 1905 is on the left. In case further emphasis were needed of the importance of the stone industry on Portland, look no more..... The hills above Fortuneswell are scarred with quarry workings, and the railway goods yard has ample quantities of stone waiting to be carried off. Given the lettering on the wagons, this picture seems to date from the pre-grouping era. PHOTOGRAPH: LENS OF SUTTON

track-bed beneath the cliffs now forms a superb footpath, albeit on Government land in a couple of places. The climb from the cliffs near Ruffs Castle towards Easton station remains largely undeveloped, although the station site itself has been built over.

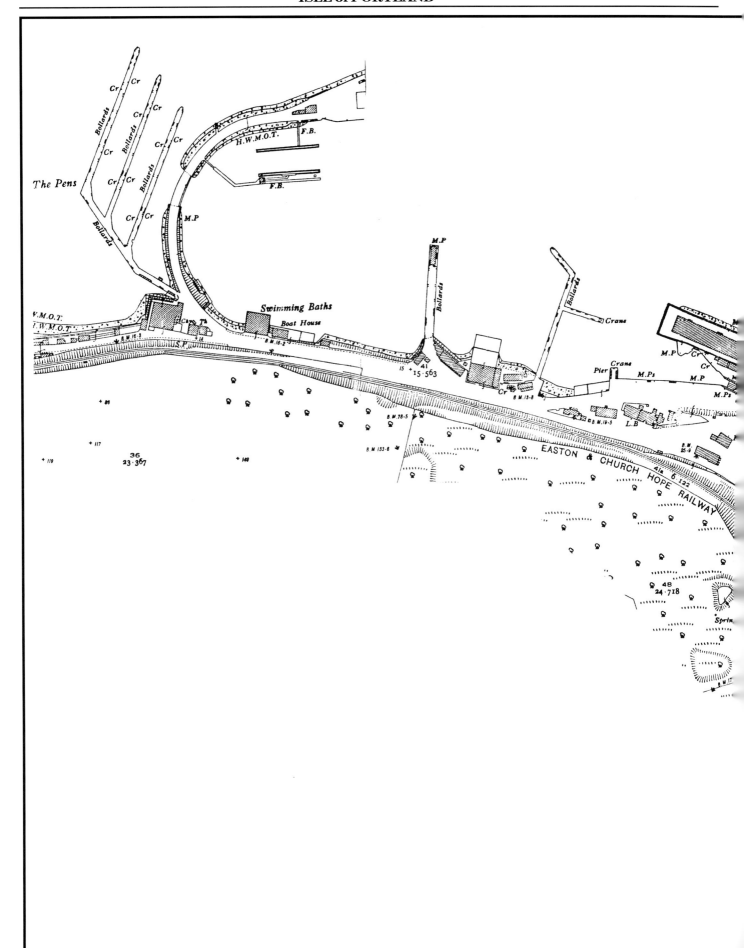

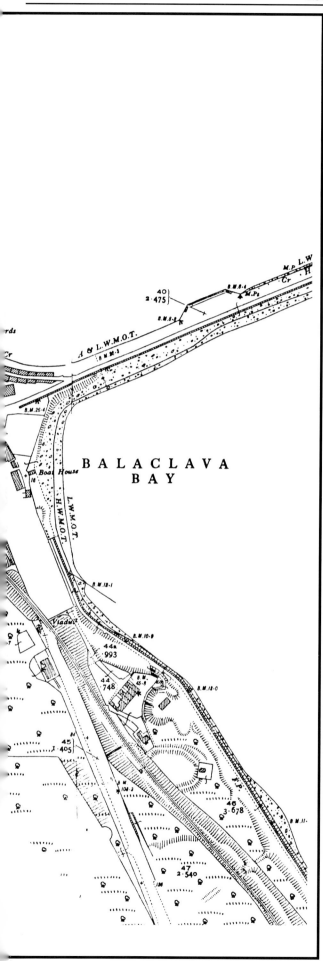

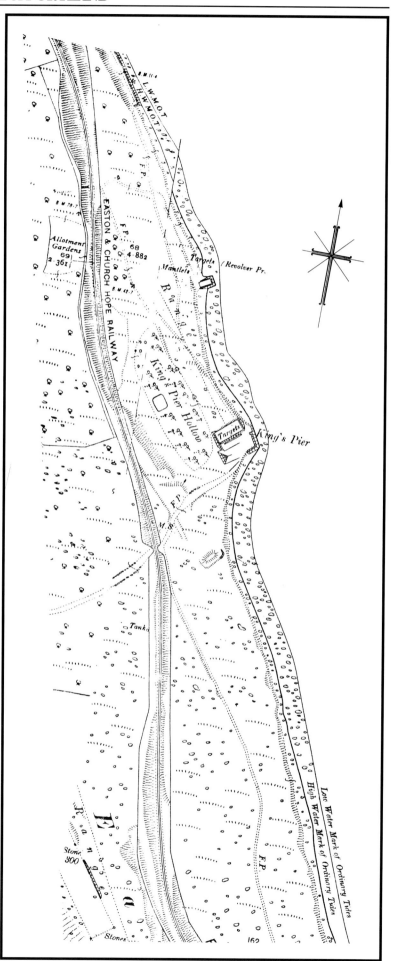

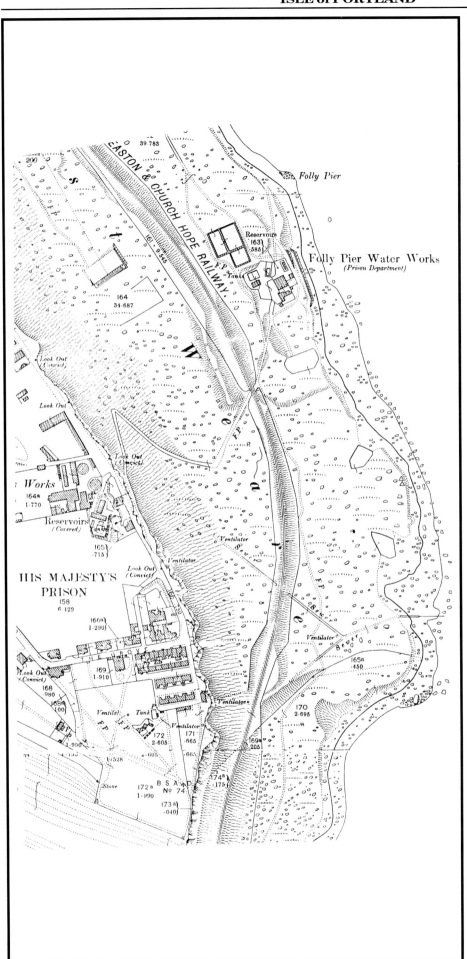

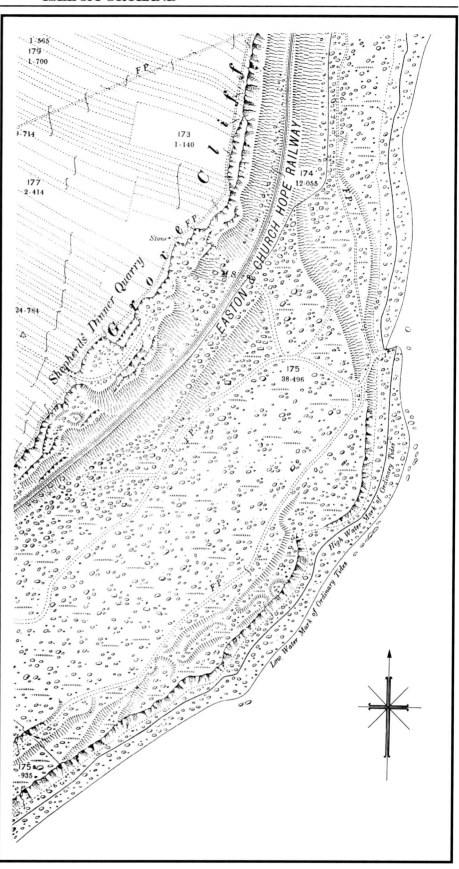

Top left. The one-time passenger terminus at Portland, 27 March 1965. Despite some sixty years of goods-only use, the platforms and buildings remained substantially unaltered. As a passenger terminus, these facilities had been far from popular..... PHOTOGRAPH: COLIN CADDY

Bottom left. The E&CH was built on a ledge at the foot of the cliffs on the east side of the Isle of Portland. The buildings on top of the cliffs in the distance (on the left) are part of the prison complex. The track-bed seen here is eminently walkable today.

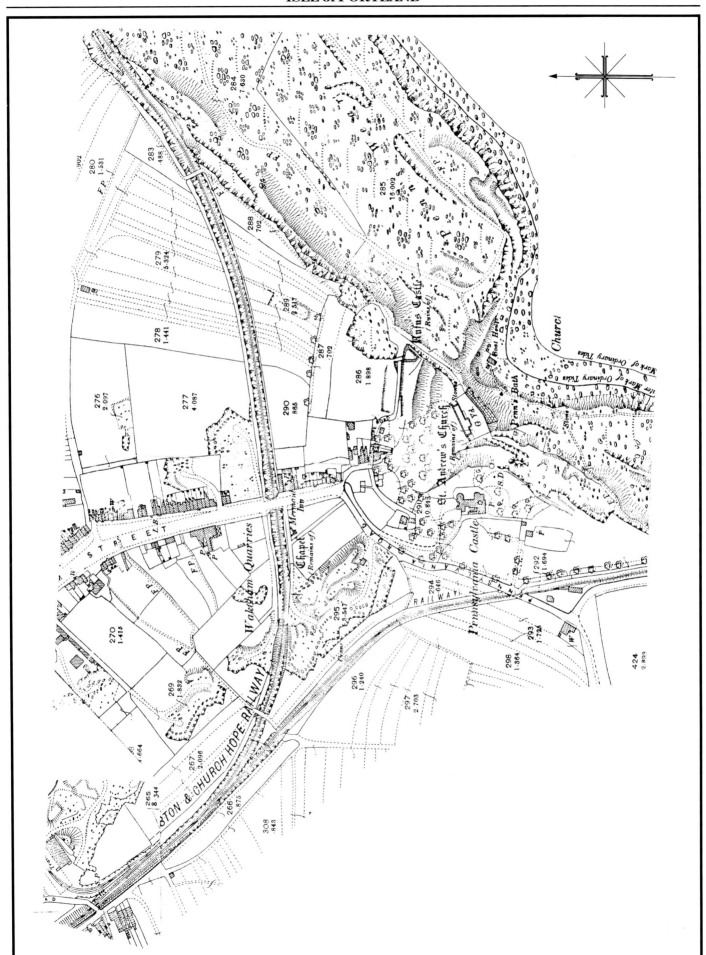

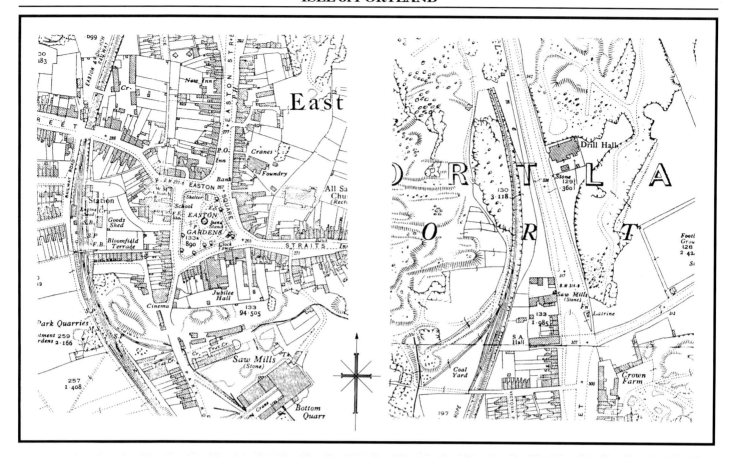

Easton station has often been described as a 'modellers prayer'. It was neat and compact, and altered very little over the years. That said, when comparing this picture to earlier ones, it is evident that the original lattice-style footbridge at the south end of the station (in the foreground here) was changed during the 1930s. This picture was taken on 29 May 1939, and shows O2 No.223 (later BR No.30223) leaving Easton with what is probably the 12.10pm departure, due at Melcombe Regis at 12.46pm. PHOTOGRAPH: R.E. TUSTIN

Above. From the 1890s until 1952, the Portland branch passenger services were usually worked by LSWR/SR O2 class 0-4-4Ts, although regular workings usually required only one locomotive. The use of two locomotives here might possibly have been because the train was a strengthened holiday excursion - but that is only a guess. This picture must have been taken after February 1935, as until then No.229 had carried the 'E' prefix (of ex-LSWR locos) - No.177 had lost the prefix in May 1933. The date can be effectively confirmed by allocation lists, which show the two locomotives to be based at Dorchester (which serviced the Portland line) from the late 1930s through to the mid-1940s. Note No.229's higher cab roof - this was a feature of the last batch of ten O2s, Nos.227-236. The location is, of course, Melcombe Regis - it can be clearly seen that, even at this comparatively late date, the original timber platform is still *in situ*. PHOTOGRAPH: LENS OF SUTTON

Below. After the cessation of passenger services in 1952 the WR 57XX 0-6-0PTs, being the regular branch goods engines, had the line virtually to themselves for more than ten years. During the spring of 1962, No.4689 prepares to leave Easton with the branch goods train for Weymouth. The remains of the engine shed lie on the right. PHOTOGRAPH: COLIN CADDY

Chapter Seven

Locomotives and Train Services

Contemporary reports state that the first Weymouth & Portland passenger train on Monday 9 October 1865 was hauled by LSWR No.154 NILE, a 2-4-0WT constructed to a Joseph Beattie design at Nine Elms Works in April 1859. 154 and two fellows had been built principally for the Waterloo - Leatherhead line, but had later gravitated to branch duties. The Portland passenger service initially comprised eleven trains each way on weekdays - these were worked by the LSWR, while goods services were operated by both the LSWR and GWR, the latter on the broad gauge.

Despite the use of NILE on the inaugural passenger train, it appears that it did not become the regular branch engine. That role fell, instead, to Beattie 'standard' 2-4-0WTs, eighty-five of which were constructed between 1862 and 1875. It is known that, from the mid-1870s to the mid-1890s (at least), one of these locomotives was usually allocated to 'Portland', although the word 'allocated' is a little deceptive in that there was no engine shed or servicing there. The 1878 and 1890 allocation lists both show No.246 at 'Portland' although it is, of course, improbable that the locomotive was there continuously throughout that period.

The Beattie standard well tanks did not have a monopoly on the line, as there is photographic evidence of a different type of locomotive at Portland in the early 1870s. The locomotive in question was No.143 NELSON, one of a class of three Beattie 2-4-0WTs built in 1858 - these had 5ft diameter driving wheels, whereas the later standard class had 5ft 6in drivers. The appearance of NELSON on the Portland branch has also been confirmed by none other than E.L. Ahrons, arguably the most lyrical railway writer of all time. As an eight year-old schoolboy on holiday at Weymouth, Ahrons cajoled the driver of NELSON into giving him his very first footplate ride - this was the unwitting start of a long and distinguished involvement with footplate matters. Of his trip on NELSON, Ahrons later wrote that it gave him: '....a somewhat superficial knowledge of certain footplate taps and handles, and a severe castigation at the hands of an irate parent who had no soul for locomotives'.

Details of the GWR locomotives which worked the Portland branch in the early days are few, but during the nine years of broad gauge operations it seems likely that Gooch's 'Standard Goods' 0-6-0s would have been among the usual types. After the elimination of the broad gauge, the archetypal 0-6-0STs took over.

As stated earlier, the original arrangement was that the GWR and LSWR were to work the passenger services on alternate years, but it seems that the GWR did not work any passenger services on the broad gauge. In standard gauge days the GWR certainly took turns on the passenger workings, as the train involved in the accident at Portland station on 23 December 1877 (see earlier) was hauled by a GWR locomotive.

For the LSWR's passenger services on the Portland branch, from around 1890 the new Adams O2 0-4-4Ts established a residency

PORTLAND STATION - passenger train traffic						
	Tickets		Tickets	Parcels		TOTAL
	issued	season	Total £	number	£	R'CPTS
1903	209,197	*	7,476	11,433	809	£ 8,285
1913	257,520	*	7,572	7,998	847	£ 8,419
1923	260,881	529	10,773	14,390	857	£11,630
1929	209,671	400	8,502	13,335	587	£ 9,089
1930	255,494	338	9,475	13,338	464	£ 9,939
1931	194,288	314	7,736	11,005	429	£ 8,165
1932	180,560	278	6,674	10,501	399	£ 7,073
1933	178,431	268	6,343	12,655	410	£ 6,753
1934	173,862	286	5,764	13,802	499	£ 6,263
1935	159,625	268	5,008	12,296	302	£ 5,310
1936	136,543	299	5,003	12,076	284	£ 5,287
1937	131,046	324	5,576	14,113	579	£ 6,155
1938	96,413	308	5,157	13,940	563	£ 5,720

* Figures not available
Includes figures for WYKE REGIS HALT (opened 1909)

Another Dorchester O2, No.30229, near Rodwell on 14 July 1951. PHOTOGRAPH: R.H. TUNSTALL

WEYMOUTH, PORTLAND, AND EASTON.

Single Line, Weymouth Junction to Portland Goods Yard Junction (crossing place, Rodwell), and from Portland Station to Easton, worked by Electric Train Staff.

DOWN TRAINS. — WEEK DAYS.

(Stations listed: Weymouth Junction dep., Melcombe Regis arr./dep., Westham, Rodwell arr./dep., Sandsfoot Castle H., Wyke Regis, Torpedo Works, Portland Goods Jct. arr./dep., Portland arr./dep., Castleton, Easton arr.)

DOWN TRAINS. — WEEK DAYS—continued. / SUNDAYS.

The Passenger Trains and Motors between Weymouth and Portland, and all Trains between Portland and Easton, will be worked by the S.R. Company until further notice.

N—Runs Portland to Easton. WSO   Z—SUSPENDED.

Weymouth, Portland, and Easton—continued.

UP TRAINS. — WEEK DAYS.

(Stations listed: Easton dep., Castleton, Portland arr./dep., Portland Goods J., Torpedo Works, Wyke Regis, Sandsfoot Castle H., Stop Board, Rodwell arr./dep., Westham, Melcombe Regis dep., Weymouth Jct. arr.)

UP TRAINS. — WEEK DAYS—continued / SUNDAYS.

D—Advertised 6.48 a.m.   Y—G.W. Engine and S.R. Guard.   Z—Suspended.   P—Will not run between Portland and Weymouth on Saturdays.

Working timetable, Summer 1939

which was to last for over sixty years. It is known that O2s Nos.214, 215 and 216 of Dorchester shed were equipped with Holt & Gresham's steam sanding gear principally for working the Portland line. In the early and mid-1890s there were usually nine passenger services each way on the Portland branch on weekdays.

In preparation for the opening of the Easton section, the Board of Trade stipulated that, given the steep gradients, goods trains on that section should be composed of no more than 10 wagons and should in all cases have two brake vans and brakesmen. Following a request by the GWR and LSWR the limit was subsequently eased to 20 loaded or empty wagons from Easton to Portland, and 14 loaded or 9 empty from Portland to Easton. For passenger trains the BoT initially recommended a maximum train weight of 4 four-wheeled carriages, but the GWR and LSWR objected to this, stating that: '....there

may be times of pressure when it would be very inconvenient to be bound to observe such a limit'. The BoT conceded, but with the strict proviso that all coaches be fitted with automatic brakes.

Following the opening of the Easton & Church Hope line to passenger traffic in 1902, the pattern of services was revised so that the entire Weymouth - Portland - Easton route was worked as a continuous line. That said, only five or six of the branch passenger trains each day actually worked right through to Easton, the others terminating at Portland.

Despite the opening through to Easton and the provision of the much-needed new station at Portland, passenger traffic on the branch was not sufficiently remunerative for the operating companies' needs. In 1908, in an attempt to attract more traffic and reduce operating costs, it was agreed that the GWR should build two high-

capacity steam railmotors for the line at a cost of £2,250 each. Steam railmotors had proved their worth elsewhere - often very emphatically - and in preparation for their arrival on the Portland branch, halts were added at Westham and Wyke Regis and a new northern 'terminus' provided at Melcombe Regis. As already emphasised, the option of branch trains starting and terminating at Melcombe Regis offered an inestimable bonus in that it dispensed with the tedious reversing arrangements into and out of Weymouth station.

In readiness for the railmotor services, Melcombe Regis station was opened in May 1909 and Westham and Wyke Regis halts in July. However, for reasons which are unclear (to this writer, at least), the GWR failed to construct the new high capacity railmotors which had been promised, and so the LSWR had to draft in one of its own 40-seat units instead. It

On 29 September 1963, BR Class 4 2-6-0 No.76057 - a type not usually associated with the Portland branch - worked a permanent way train to the site of Sandsfoot Castle halt, where there had been a subsidence. PHOTOGRAPH: COLIN CADDY

PORTLAND STATION - goods train traffic										
	FORWARDED - tons			RECEIVED - tons			'not charged' (tons)	TOTAL GOODS (tons)	TOTAL GOODS £	L-stck Vans
	Coal & Coke	Other minerals	General	Coal & Coke	Other minerals	General				
1903	252	12,515	945	4,157	14,301	3,079	10,227	45,476	11,696	200
1913	22	6,367	550	2,327	423	4,197	2,382	16,268	8,877	136
1923	45	13,546	801	430	444	2,371	4,930	22,567	17,028	5
1929	590	14,929	2,073	1,109	373	1,972	3,471	24,517	19,581	-
1930	246	15,881	1,587	1,241	570	2,038	3,054	24,617	19,462	-
1931	199	18,031	1,756	910	648	2,018	3,680	27,242	21,998	1
1932	321	15,658	299	579	408	1,465	3,124	21,854	17,184	1
1933	308	9,553	175	480	595	1,588	2,837	15,536	10,726	-
1934	313	5,683	161	830	366	1,680	3,886	12,919	8,402	-
1935	169	7,440	225	1,134	528	2,095	3,724	15,315	10,945	-
1936	37	7,040	178	807	283	1,934	2,716	12,995	9,714	-
1937	17	6,174	296	257	451	2,238	3,931	13,364	10,075	-
1938	13	4,935	543	145	145	3,082	4,480	13,343	11,259	-

To cope with the anticipated demand on the last Saturday of scheduled passenger services, the Portland branch train was formed of six WR corridor coaches and hauled by O2s Nos.30177 and 30197. Having arrived at Melcombe Regis with the 1.53pm from Easton, the train pulls forward to Weymouth Junction where the locomotives will run round in readiness to work the 2.35pm Melcombe Regis - Easton. PHOTOGRAPH: S.C. NASH

commenced work on the Portland branch on 1 September 1909, and although it helped to attract additional traffic, there were drawbacks. As elsewhere, it was found that the branch railmotor could not always cope with early morning and evening peak time demand. A conventional locomotive-hauled train could be strengthened with another carriage if required, but this was not possible with the railmotor. After only four months, locomotive hauled trains had to be reinstated on the Portland branch.

The tried and tested O2 0-4-4Ts returned to the branch, and during the summer of 1911 Nos.202, 214, 233 and 234 were engaged on the line at various times. LSWR coal returns for August 1911 (as quoted by D.L. Bradley in his book *LSWR Locomotives*) indicate that No.233 was the most regular Portland branch engine that month, covering 1,950 miles on passenger duties and 333 on goods, and consuming a somewhat gluttonous average of 42lb of coal per mile.

By the early 1920s the usual pattern was for the LSWR to work the passenger services and the GWR the goods. During the summer of 1922 - the last before the grouping, incidentally - the branch passenger services consisted of 18 trains from Melcombe Regis to Portland on weekdays and 19 in the opposite direction. Of these, five in each direction continued through to/from Easton. There was an additional late evening train each way between Melcombe Regis and Portland on Saturdays. The journey times were 16 minutes between Melcombe Regis and Portland, or around 35 minutes through to/from Easton. The Sunday service comprised seven each way between Melcombe Regis and Portland only. At this period, the first and last passenger trains each weekday started/terminated at Melcombe Regis - that is, they were worked from the Weymouth end, by LSWR locomotives from Weymouth shed. One might therefore query whether the little engine shed at Easton had any real purpose in life at this time, for according to the official GWR allocation registers there were no GWR locomotives allocated to Easton shed for the first weeks of the railway year in 1923, 1924 and 1925. Hazarding a guess, if any locomotive were actually outstationed at Easton during that period, it might have been an LSWR/SR one, for use on local shunting duties.

During the alterations to Weymouth station in the latter half of the 1930s, the SR engine shed on the east side of the station closed. Consequently, from January 1939 a couple of Dorchester locomotives - invariably O2s - were sub-shedded at the GWR depot at Weymouth, their principal duties being the Portland branch passenger services. Dorchester shed had two booked turns for its own O2s, one of which was the Dorchester - Portland - Easton goods.

By this time, the Easton section was served by only five passenger trains each way on weekdays and six on Saturdays. As an experimental economy measure, for the winter of 1937/38 the

8.33am ex-Melcombe Regis terminated at Portland instead of continuing to Easton (with the consequent loss of the 9.30am ex-Easton), while on Mondays-Fridays the 12.09pm ex-Melcombe Regis also terminated at Portland instead of Easton (thereby cancelling out the 1.25pm ex-Easton). The experiment was considered satisfactory, and the reduction in services became permanent.

Given the importance of the Naval base at Portland, it was inevitable that the Portland branch saw a considerable increase in strategic traffic during the war. Special trains for Naval personnel became fairly commonplace; these sometimes comprised up to ten corridor coaches and were double headed. Among the locomotive types used on these workings were Q and 700 class 0-6-0s, T9 and K10 4-4-0s, and GWR 43XX 2-6-0s. Frustratingly, precise details of specific Naval special workings are few and far between. One of the few specific reports concerns a Naval special to Portland on 19 November 1941, which was double-headed by K10 No.387 and T9 No.284, both of Dorchester shed.

There is a story about a GWR Hall 4-6-0 being rostered to work a Navy special, only to lose its cylinder casing on the platform edge at Portland. That story is, however, very much unconfirmed, although the prospect of a large outside-cylinder GWR locomotive having clearance problems at Portland is in itself quite fea-

B168	**Engine Restrictions**—continued		
	Branches—continued		
Section of Line	Route Colour	Engines Authorised	Local Prohibitions
Weymouth, Portland and Easton ...	Yellow	51XX between Weymouth Junction and Melcombe Regis at maximum speed of twenty-five miles per hour. 45XX and 55XX Weymouth to Portland only and not over Dock Yard Sidings. 43XX, 53XX, 63XX, 73XX, 78XX and B.R. Standard, Class 2 (2-6-0), B.R. Standard, Class 4 (4-6-0), Weymouth to Portland Station only, and not to exceed speed of twenty-five miles per hour at any point. All "Yellow" and uncoloured engines without outside cylinders. "Red" Group Engines Nos. 40XX, 50XX, 68XX, 49XX, 59XX, 69XX, 79XX, 10XX, 78XX, 40XX (Star), 43XX, B.R. Standard, Class 7 (4-6-2) and S.R. Classes, H15, N15 and S15 are permitted to work on passenger trains from the Weymouth direction, terminating at Melcombe Regis and may be allowed, when working passenger trains, to draw up on the bridge known as Backwater Viaduct.	

Engine restrictions, taken from WR working timetable for summer 1955.

Top. **Crossing the Chesil - O2 No.30229 hauls the former Isle of Sheppey articulated set which had been transferred to the Portland branch after the Sheppey line's closure in December 1950. The date is 14 July 1951 and the train is the 4.55pm Portland - Melcombe Regis. Portland Dockyard can be seen in the distance on the left. PHOTOGRAPH: R.H. TUNSTALL**

Below. **O2 No.30197 leaves Westham halt with the 11.30am Portland - Melcombe Regis on 10 July 1951. PHOTOGRAPH: R.H. TUNSTALL**

EASTON STATION - passenger train traffic						
	Tickets		Tickets	Parcels		TOTAL
	issued	season	£	number	£	R'CPTS
1929	1,080	-	304	5,621	174	£ 478
1930	895	-	237	5,853	135	£ 372
1931	954	-	431	5,557	132	£ 563
1932	711	-	109	4,742	116	£ 225
1933	1,274	-	223	5,963	119	£ 342
1934	736	-	187	5,902	100	£ 287
1935	529	-	158	5,465	43	£ 201
1936	711	-	219	5,302	60	£ 279
1937	351	-	164	6,808	49	£ 213
1938	637	-	325	5,277	60	£ 385

sible. On the subject of whether or not a Hall worked to Portland, GWR devotees will be quick to point to a discrepancy in route availability - the Portland branch was categorised 'Yellow' (i.e. it was considered suitable only for locomotives with axle weights of 16 tons or less), but the Halls, having a maximum axle weight of 18 tons 19 cwt, were firmly in the 'Red' route availability category. That said, things weren't always as cut and dried as might be imagined. The SR T9s, K10s, Qs and 700s - which are known to have visited Portland - *all* had axle weights in excess of 16 tons.

The report referring to the workings of 19 November 1941, incidentally, also quoted Dorchester's O2s Nos.177, 223, 229 and 233 as being in charge of the Portland motor and freight trains, albeit with a GWR 48XX (later 14XX) 0-4-2T looking after one morning passenger trip and a pannier tank looking after a morning freight trip. The reported use of a 48XX on the Portland branch is especially interesting. In 1941 Weymouth shed had three of these 0-4-2Ts - Nos.4815, 4854 and 4867 (later 1415, 1454, 1467 respectively) - for auto duties, but their activities were usually confined to the Abbotsbury branch and the Weymouth - Yeovil locals.

Another report filed during the war commented about the Portland branch being worked by an O2 and 'a pair of GW auto coaches'. If that report was accurate, it undoubtedly referred to the O2 *hauling* the GW trailers - *not* working in conventional auto/motor train mode. The Dorchester O2s were not motor fitted - they ran round their trains at Easton or Portland - but even if they had been motor fitted, they would not have been compatible with GW auto train stock.

A typical wartime public timetable - this one is for the period commencing May 1943 - shows nine each way between Melcombe Regis and Portland on weekdays (seven on Sundays) and three each way between Melcombe Regis and Easton. The usual journey times were 14 or 15 minutes between Melcombe Regis and Portland (4 miles) and 11 or 12 minutes between Portland and Easton (3½ miles). A visitor to the line on 12 May 1943 reported that O2s Nos.177 and 233 were in charge of the branch passenger services while GWR 27XX class 0-6-0PT No.2720 was looking after the goods workings. A couple of years or so later - on 25 July 1945 - another visit to the line revealed O2 No.177 on the branch passenger train and a second O2, No.229, shunting at Easton. At this time,

the Portland - Easton section was served by only three passenger trains each way on weekdays. There was no Sunday service on that section.

During the summer of 1947, the weekday branch services comprised twelve passenger trains each way between Melcombe Regis and Portland and six between Melcombe Regis and Easton. On Sundays, there were seven advertised trains plus one unadvertised working each way between Melcombe Regis and Portland - there were no trains to/from Easton on Sundays. Of the weekday services, the 10.25pm ex-Melcombe Regis was advertised to run non-stop to Portland in 10 minutes - the return working from Portland at 10.46pm was also non-stop, albeit with a more sedate allowance of 14 minutes. The scheduled goods workings (weekdays only) seemed rather meagre - one GWR working to Portland and return and one SR working to Easton and return. Appearances were, however, often deceptive as the goods trains were usually well loaded - the principal traffics were stone from Easton, Naval supplies to and from Portland, and goods to/from the Torpedo Works at Wyke Regis. By this time the passenger trains were usually formed of three or four GWR corridor coaches. The frequency of branch passenger services was somewhat misleading, as outside the peak business times the trains were often very sparsely used. There was little chance of the branch attracting anything other than local traffic, as the branch trains ran only to/from Melcombe Regis, not to the main station at Weymouth.

The public timetable for the period commencing 6 October 1947 - the very last timetable before Nationalisation - showed a reduction in weekday services. Three return trips between Melcombe Regis and Portland had been discontinued. These were:

9.57am ex-Melcombe Regis, 11.03am ex-Portland
11.53am ex-Melcombe Regis, 12.53pm ex-Portland
5.35pm ex-Melcombe Regis, 6.03pm ex-Portland

Also, one of the six return trips to Easton became a 'Saturdays Only' working - this was the 6.33pm Melcombe Regis and 7.10pm ex-Easton.

Following the withdrawal of scheduled passenger services as from Monday 3 March 1952, the branch remained open for goods workings -

usually two trains each way on weekdays. The scheduled goods workings listed in the summer 1954 Working Timetable were:

1) Dep. Weymouth Junction 8.58am; arr. Portland 9.17am. Dep. Portland 10.25am; arr. Weymouth Junction 11.06am.

2) Dep. Weymouth Junction 11.30am; arr. Easton 1.10pm. Dep. Easton 2.25pm; arr. Weymouth Junction 4.11pm. (In each direction, this train was allowed about an hour at Portland).

These trains were usually worked by WR 57XX 0-6-0PTs, which were considered to have a greater reserve of power than the O2s. Here, again, there was a discrepancy in route availability - as explained earlier, the Portland branch was categorised 'Yellow', but the 57XXs had maximum axleweights of 16 tons 15 cwt which should, in theory, placed them in the heavier 'Blue' category. The fact of the matter was that the 57XXs *were* originally categorised 'Blue', but in 1950 were recategorised 'Yellow'. This was solely a reflection of their very modest hammer blow, and not through any weight-saving modifications.

As already mentioned, on summer Saturdays in the 1950s empty coaching stock was sometimes berthed at the Melcombe Regis end of the branch, not only at the station itself, but also on Backwater Viaduct. There are unconfirmed reports of stock also being stored at Portland station yard, and it has been suggested that, in the early 1950s, Bulleid light Pacifics were occasionally used to take the empty stock to Portland and back. However, this writer has a sneaking suspicion that somebody observed empty stock being taken to Melcombe Regis, and mistakenly assumed that it was continuing to Portland. Can any reader confirm one way or the other?

Referring to the possibility of Bulleid Pacifics going to Portland on empty stock duties - but without wishing to turn this section into a discourse on locomotive axle weights and route availability - it should be pointed out that the light Pacifics, in their original unrebuilt form, had maximum axle weights of 18 tons 15 cwt. This was, of course, in excess of the official weight limit for the branch, but as we have already seen, such an obstacle wasn't necessarily insurmountable.

On two occasions in the 1950s, the branch was traversed by enthusiasts' specials. The first was on 8 July 1956 when, as part of the RCTS 334 mile-long 'Wessex Wyvern' railtour, 0-6-0PT No.4624 hauled a three-coach train of LSWR stock from Melcombe Regis to Easton

EASTON STATION - goods train traffic									
	FORWARDED - tons			RECEIVED - tons			'not charged' (tons)	TOTAL GOODS (tons)	TOTAL GOODS £
	Coal & Coke	Other minerals	General	Coal & Coke	Other minerals	General			
1903	-	8,411	119	2,128	1,161	653	1,067	13,539	2,533
1913	-	10,475	229	2,032	519	768	2,994	17,017	6,870
1923	-	6,519	378	2,043	440	1,132	2,986	13,498	9,294
1929	-	11,006	367	1,968	522	1,525	3,551	18,939	13,646
1930	-	20,649	311	1,627	375	1,350	3,512	27,869	18,352
1931	11	15,197	345	1,287	73	1,259	3,176	21,348	10,463
1932	-	13,533	327	1,016	163	1,015	3,125	19,179	10,514
1933	-	7,914	252	661	180	562	2,382	11,951	4,989
1934	-	6,403	231	731	291	649	2,398	10,703	7,771
1935	-	4,544	241	830	299	718	2,603	9,235	6,616
1936	-	4,534	297	953	200	822	2,484	9,290	6,710
1937	-	5,609	294	1,264	101	902	2,301	10,471	8,312
1938	-	2,807	342	783	138	1,009	2,387	7,466	5,773

and return, stopping, in time honoured fashion, for photo calls *en route*. The second railtour of the decade took place on 7 June 1958 when a Railway Enthusiasts' Club special visited the line through to Easton. The locomotive was M7 0-4-4T No.30107 (a type rarely - if ever - seen on the branch in ordinary service) and the train was formed of LSWR motor set No.738.

There was another special working on 29 April 1959, but this one was a little different. The occasion was the visit of HM The Queen to the Naval Base at Portland - the Royal Train was worked from Weymouth to Portland and back by WR 0-6-0PTs Nos.3737 and 4689, suitably spruced up for the occasion.

At Melcombe Regis, the disused station was frequently used as a peak season 'overflow' for the main line station, and although most of the 'diverted' trains were locals or excursions, it was not unknown for longer-distance trains to be routed there. Consequently, WR 4-6-0s - Halls, Granges and on at least one occasion a Castle - brought trains into Melcombe Regis. This was indeed a major elevation in status for the humble little station.

During the spring and summer of 1959, the goods station at Portland (the one-time passenger terminus) was put to use as a sorting point for Channel Islands goods traffic. Weymouth had gained some of Southampton Channel Island traffic, but the need for checking, sorting and documentation of cargo before shipment had caused congestion which inevitably resulted in delays. The previous summer, Melcombe Regis had been used as a staging point for this traffic, but that had been viewed only as a makeshift solution. As from 27 April 1959, the unchecked Channel Islands wagons were taken across to Portland where the loads could be prepared for immediate shipment on return to Weymouth Quay. For this arrangement, an additional daily

goods train to/from Portland had to be laid on - it left Weymouth at 4.30pm with unchecked wagons, returning about an hour later with the previous day's quota of checked cargo. The train was usually formed of twenty-five wagons - the maximum permitted on the Portland branch.

Those goods workings were handled almost exclusively by WR 0-6-0PTs, as were the ordinary goods services to Portland and Easton. The GWR's own loading limits for most types of pannier tanks on the branch were: Weymouth - Portland 176 tons; Portland - Weymouth 193 tons; Portland - Easton 118 tons; Easton - Portland 176 tons. The pannier tank hegemony continued until the autumn of 1963 when Weymouth's last eight representatives were displaced by six Ivatt 2-6-2Ts. The Ivatts inherited the Portland branch goods workings - their other duties included banking at Bincombe (between Weymouth and Dorchester) but, on the whole, they were not over-used.

Probably the last high-profile Portland duties undertaken by Weymouth's pannier tanks was the working of an enthusiasts' special to Easton on 25 August 1963. The train, comprising seven corridor coaches, was worked by Nos.4689 and 7782, one at either end of the train.

There was another enthusiasts' special on 27 March 1965 - this train had an Ivatt tank at each end (one was No.41284).

By this time, the branch line was nearing the very end of its life. Indeed, since June 1964 the goods services between Portland and Easton had run only when required. The end came on 5 April 1965 when the scheduled goods workings to Portland were withdrawn.

Below. **From June 1964, the branch goods services ran beyond Portland only when required. On 6 February 1965, Ivatt tank No.41293 with a van and an open for Easton approach Castle Road bridge. PHOTOGRAPH: COLIN CADDY**

RODWELL STATION (passenger traffic only)						
	Tickets		Tickets	Parcels		TOTAL
	issued	season	£	number	£	R'CPTS
1903	77,612	*	1,386	446	30	£ 1,416
1913	134,946	*	1,734	1,140	34	£ 1,768
1923	88,263	398	2,287	777	27	£ 2,314
1929	87,943	320	1,840	399	19	£ 1,859
1930	90,016	253	1,822	374	7	£ 1,829
1931	76,431	237	1,681	378	4	£ 1,685
1932	67,159	210	1,452	398	4	£ 1,456
1933	60,336	196	1,289	423	2	£ 1,291
1934	70,995	159	1,289	393	3	£ 1,292
1935	80,803	156	1,343	325	2	£ 1,345
1936	88,242	185	1,375	249	2	£ 1,377
1937	95,253	165	1,450	250	6	£ 1,456
1938	81,705	128	1,404	198	6	£ 1,410
* Figures not available						

MELCOMBE REGIS STATION (passenger traffic only)						
	Tickets		Tickets	Parcels		TOTAL
	issued	season	£	number	£	R'CPTS
1913	309,561	*	3,570	5,794	174	£ 3,744
1923	198,451	*	4,405	4,210	207	£ 4,612
1929	212,993	243	4,449	1,926	120	£ 4,569
1930	229,484	215	5,134	1,738	111	£ 5,245
1931	208,575	164	4,606	1,209	88	£ 4,694
1932	196,266	125	4,279	1,321	83	£ 4,362
1933	193,203	109	4,022	1,086	75	£ 4,097
1934	235,645	122	4,666	851	63	£ 4,729
1935	248,924	123	4,666	953•	64	£ 4,730
1936	264,830	140	4,870	859	54	£ 4,924
1937	292,675	147	5,437	814	53	£ 5,490
1938	256,199	141	5,134	897	48	£ 5,182
* Figures not available Includes figures for WESTHAM HALT